All About Azaleas, Camellias & Rhododendrons

Created and designed by
the editorial staff of
ORTHO BOOKS

Writers
Derek Fell
Fred Galle

Designer
Gary Hespenheide

Ortho Books

Publisher
Robert B. Loperena

Editorial Director
Christine Jordan

Manufacturing Director
Ernie S. Tasaki

Managing Editor
Sally W. Smith

Editor
Robert J. Beckstrom

Prepress Supervisor
Linda M. Bouchard

Editorial Assistants
Joni Christiansen
Sally J. French

Address all inquiries to
Ortho Books
Box 5006
San Ramon, CA 94583-0906

Copyright © 1985, 1995
Monsanto Company
All rights reserved under international and Pan-American copyright conventions.

2 3 4 5 6 7 8 9
97 98 99 2000

ISBN 0-89721-257-6
Library of Congress Catalog Card
Number 94-69602

THE SOLARIS GROUP
2527 Camino Ramon
San Ramon, CA 94583-0906

Endorsements

Speaking on behalf of the Board of Directors of the Azalea Society of America, I would like to fully endorse this fine book *All About Azaleas, Camellias & Rhododendrons.* The information contained within will be most helpful to azalea enthusiasts throughout the country and a welcome addition to anyone's library.

William C. Miller III
The Azalea Society of America

The American Camellia Society wholeheartedly endorses *All About Azaleas, Camellias & Rhododendrons.* Camellias bring pleasure to one's life and this book shows how to grow these beautiful plants to perfection.

Ann Blair Brown
Executive Director
The American Camellia Society

The American Rhododendron Society endorses *All About Azaleas, Camellias & Rhododendrons* as a valuable contribution towards greater understanding and appreciation of these garden aristocrats.

A. Richard Brooks
President
The American Rhododendron Society

Acknowledgments

Illustrators
Tony Davis
Ron Hildebrand

Editorial Coordinator
Cass Dempsey

Consultants
The American Camellia Society
The American Rhododendron Society
The Azalea Society of America

Copyeditor
Toni Murray

Proofreader
Alicia K. Eckley

Indexer
Trisha Lamb Feuerstein

Special Thanks to
Deborah Cowder
David Van Ness

Color Separations by
Color Tech. Corp.

Lithographed in the USA by
Banta Company

Primary Photographer
Harold Greer

Additional Photographers
Names of photographers are followed by the page numbers on which their work appears.
R = right, C = center, L = left, T = top, B = bottom

R. Adkins: 45L
American Camellia Society: 13BL, 81L, 84L, 84R, 87C
Laurie Black: 8T, 20T, 90R
R. H. Brame: 42T
Barstow Bridges: 42B
Richard Christman: 45B
J. Coartney: 45R
Spencer Davis: 43R
Michael Dirr: 45C
Derek Fell: 12B, 14BL, 18, 24, 50, 56L, 56R, 58R, 63R, 67L, 79L, 86R
Fred Galle: 7L, 9T, 53L, 63L, 64L, 64R, 65L, 66L, 69L, 71R, 74R, 79R
Duane Hatch: 42R
Saxon Holt: front cover, 1, 4–5, 11T, 11B, 20B, 28, 46, 51L, 58L, 79C
Ray Kriner: 43L
OIS Stock Files: 15, 43C
Pam Peirce: 13TL, 13LC, 23, 43TL, 54L, 55R, 62R, 80R, 82BL, 82TR, 82BR, 83L, 83R, 85L, 85R, 86L, 87L, 87R, 88L, 88BR, 89L, 89R, 90L, 91L, 91R, back cover BL
Charles Powell: 44C
Michael Smith: 42L
Herbert Spady: 44BL, 44R

Front Cover
This quiet retreat is warmed with a profusion of azaleas.

Title Page
Rhododendrons are prized for their enthusiastic growth as well as their spectacular blossoms.

Back Cover
Top Left: This is *Rhododendron keiskei,* a species native to Japan.
Top Right: *Rhododendron zoelleri* is a vireya rhododendron, a native of New Guinea that, unfortunately, is a greenhouse specimen anyplace that freezes in the winter.
Bottom Left: Like other sansanqua camellias, 'Jean May' begins blooming in the fall, extending the camellia season to the other half of the year.
Bottom Right: 'Queen Whilhelmina', a deciduous azalea, is hardier than evergreen azaleas, allowing azaleas to be grown as far north as the Great Lakes region.

All About Azaleas, Camellias & Rhododendrons

Introducing Azaleas, Rhododendrons, and Camellias

Their spectacular flowers, beautiful foliage, and attractive form place rhododendrons, azaleas, and camellias among the most popular ornamental plants.

Rhododendrons, azaleas, and camellias are prized as ornamental shrubs the world over. Their popularity is well deserved; the beautiful blooms rival those of any other plant. Rhododendrons are renowned for their spectacular and dramatic flower clusters; azaleas for their vibrant displays of color; and camellias for their perfectly formed, iridescent blossoms. These plants offer much more than blossoms, however; other qualities include handsome foliage, a variety of shapes and sizes, and versatility in the landscape.

In spite of the fact that, botanically speaking, rhododendrons and azaleas (which are both in the genus *Rhododendron*) are from a distinctly different plant family than camellias, they are all similar in many respects. They relish moist, slightly acid, humus-rich, and well-drained soil. From a distance some even look alike (glossy, dark, evergreen leaves and shrubby habit) and have many of the same uses in the landscape. For all three, the largest concentration of species is in a triangle of Asia that includes Nepal, parts of southwestern China, and northern Burma. In particular, the provinces of Yunnan and Szechwan in western China are a treasury of rhododendron and camellia species.

Hybridizers have selected many of these species as breeding stock to develop exciting new hybrid rhododendrons, azaleas, and camellias. Many of these hybrids are able to withstand winter temperatures below 0° F.

The combination of rhododendrons and azaleas makes a striking collage of color.

RHODODENDRONS AND AZALEAS

Although a few rhododendrons have been cultivated for a long time, azaleas have the more rich and lengthy history. Finely textured and delicate, many species of azaleas have been cultivated by the Japanese for centuries. Azaleas were first mentioned in a Japanese book of poems in AD 759 and have held a revered place in Japanese gardens, thought, and lore ever since. Japanese azaleas were introduced to China and Asia following the early pilgrimages of Buddhist monks. Many of the early azaleas introduced to Europe were cultivated plants collected from gardens in China and Japan, rather than species taken from the wild.

By comparison, most rhododendrons have been in cultivation for a relatively short period of time. These striking plants stirred the imaginations of many plant collectors, who mounted daring expeditions in search of new varieties. So strong was the urge to possess rhododendrons that adventurers journeyed far into the wilderness areas of the Himalayas, sponsored by bankers, industrialists, and British aristocrats intent on creating unique collections.

The world's highest mountains, the awesome Himalayas, stretch for more than 1,500 miles in a great arc across the top of India. It is a fearsome landmass, providing a vast range of microclimates for a remarkable variety of plants. Tropical rain forests on the lower slopes, where exotic tree ferns and orchids flourish, gradually change to treeless snow ridges and alpine meadows where only the hardiest plants can survive.

Between 2,000 and 18,000 feet, the rhododendron is king. This area contains two thirds of the world's eight hundred rhododendron species. The valleys are shrouded in mist for much of the year. Under these ideal conditions, tree rhododendrons grow to monstrous proportions. Frank Kingdon–Ward, one of the most determined of the plant explorers who crisscrossed these forbidding regions in the 1920s and 1930s, described a rhododendron he saw on the Tibetan–Burmese frontier as 55 feet high and 6 feet in diameter. It bore eight hundred trusses of shimmering red flowers as big as soccer balls.

At 8,000 feet the rhododendrons are so thick and tall that they dominate the ecosystem. Although some are poisonous, many are not and their flowers provide food for monkeys. Birds feast on their nectar, and bears find refuge in the tangle of stems and branches. The musk deer in the rhododendron forest are hornless so they can wander uninhibited through the thickets. Huge leeches live in the humid overhead canopy, dropping on all

The color impact of a mass planting of azaleas is so spectacular in the spring that it can make a garden's reputation.

intruders. Until the advent of modern pesticides, leech infestations were so severe at certain times of the year that native guides would refuse to enter the dark rhododendron forest.

At 12,000 to 18,000 feet, where the conifer forest gives way to scrub, the rhododendrons become prostrate and have smaller flowers, more like the heaths and heathers to which they are related. In these locations, the plants—many of them with narrower leaves and strong fragrance—carpet the ground for miles and miles.

A large number of beautiful rhododendron species are found in tropical climates, notably New Guinea, Malaysia, and the Philippines. There is even a species that somehow found a home in Australia. None have been found in either Africa or South America, but there are a few in Europe, particularly in the Alps. North America has a significant number of species—around twenty—including those rhododendrons classified as azaleas.

Native American azalea species are all deciduous and bear flowers that are mostly white, pink, or red. Individual flowers are smaller than those of rhododendrons, but the mass effect can be impressive. However, they possess one important trait lacking in Himalayan rhododendrons—*hardiness.* The hardy native species are found among the Appalachian Mountains from Maine to Georgia, and along the coastal slopes of California and the Pacific Northwest. Many of the tender Himalayan rhododendrons have been crossed with native species, capturing desirable colors in hardy offspring suitable for some of the coldest North American climates.

CAMELLIAS

The home of the camellia is China and the lands that border China to the east, west, and south, including parts of India, Burma, Korea, Formosa, and Japan. The native habitat of the camellia is a picturesque world of gently sloping wooded hillsides and sparse forests. In misty valleys with damp, humus-rich soil, camellias grow into stately, moss-covered trees over 30 feet high with smooth, gray trunks more than a foot thick.

To the ancient Chinese the camellia plant produced the ideal flowers—smooth, flat petals; rounded form; perfect symmetry; and a conspicuous ring of powdery golden stamens clustered at the center. The revered camellia was a favorite flower to paint, to cup in the hands to ponder its blemish-free beauty, to float on the surface of water, and to adorn the secret gardens of the emperors. Some camellia trees were so sacred to these ancient Chinese that it was forbidden to take a cutting or even to gather their seeds.

Left: The flame azalea, a native of the Appalachians, is hardy to −15° F. Right: Camellias have long been cherished for their refinement and delicacy. This is 'Nuccio's Gem'.

In the wild, camellias are successful understory plants, finding good company in shady tall oaks and other durable deciduous trees. In forest clearings they form "forests within a forest." Indeed, Descanso Gardens, just north of Los Angeles, presents a realistic replica of a primeval forest, and it contains many acres of magnificent camellias threaded with trails and shaded by magnificent California live oaks.

Although the huge floral clusters (trusses) of rhododendrons are showier, camellias have always been more expensive, more refined as a garden plant, more cherished and pampered, and surrounded with a slightly more sophisticated aura. Like the rose, the camellia has strong romantic associations; it is a symbol of love and purity.

RHODODENDRONS, AZALEAS, AND CAMELLIAS IN THE LANDSCAPE

The advantages of rhododendrons, azaleas, and camellias are similar to those of other landscape plants. They tend to be long-lived woody evergreens that make reliable permanent plantings and can effectively establish the

Top: With glistening leaves and classical flowers, camellias make a classic arrangement of cut flowers.
Bottom: Rhododendrons and azaleas, with their masses of blossoms, are dramatic landscape accents. This deciduous azalea, 'Queen Wilhelmina', is at the height of bloom.

Terminology

On a superficial level it may be adequate simply to know the difference between a rhododendron, an azalea, and a camellia. Knowing some of the specialized terms used to discuss these plants can lead to a better understanding, however.

Blotch A darker colored spot that sometimes occurs on the top upright petal of rhododendrons.

Clone The name applied to a plant propagated asexually so that it is genetically identical to its parent. Clones are produced from cuttings, layering, grafting, or tissue culture, but not ever from seeds.

Cultivar A group of cultivated plants, such as 'Pink Cameo' or 'Betty Sheffield', with distinguishable characteristics (for example, a particular flower color or growth habit) that differ from those of the normal form of the plant. When reproduced, cultivars retain these characteristics. The term is derived from *CULTIvated VARiety*.

Elepidote Meaning without scales, the word *elepidote* denotes a group of rhododendrons that have no scales on the leaf undersides.

Hybrid An interspecific hybrid is a plant produced by crossing two different species, such as *Rhododendron carolinianum* with *R. dauricum* to produce the hybrid 'P.J.M.' An intraspecific hybrid is one produced by crossing different plants of a species.

Indumentum The woolly or hairy covering on the leaf surface is called indumentum. This is particularly noticeable on *Rhododendron yakushimanum*. Densely matted hairs are also called tomentum.

Lepidote The word *lepidote* means scales and refers to a group of rhododendrons with tiny scales on the undersides of the leaves.

Lobe A lobe is the rounded division of a flower.

Species A species is a basic unit of classification used to designate groups of plants (and animals) that are recognizable as distinct and can freely interbreed among themselves.

Sport A sport is a spontaneous plant mutation, usually appearing as a shoot with flowers or colors different from those on the rest of the plant.

Truss The flower cluster of a rhododendron is called a truss.

Variety A variety is a naturally occurring variation of a wild species. For example the rhododendron *R. thomsonii* var. *pallida* is the pale form of the species *R. thomsonii*. *Variety* is often used in the same way as *cultivar*.

The floral displays of azaleas and rhododendrons differ. Flowers of the azalea Rhododendron bakeri *(top) are in small clusters; the rhododendron 'Roseum Elegans' (bottom) has large trusses.*

framework of a garden. Most are tolerant of shade, have extremely showy blooms (not at all common in shade-loving plants), and have attractive foliage that is ornamental even when the plants are not in bloom. Above all, they are versatile plants that can be used to create many desirable design features in a garden.

Used alone, a prime specimen rhododendron can make a dramatic lawn highlight, especially when ringed with ferns. Massed in a row, rhododendrons can tolerate crowding to create hedges, screens, and windbreaks to line driveways, delineate vistas, and form corridors as a transition from one garden area to another.

Azaleas make their best color statement in a mass and are especially lovely when reflected in the surface of a lake. You can "paint" a landscape with azaleas, like daubing a canvas with solid brushstrokes. They are spectacular when planted informally in solid sheets of color across a shaded slope or closer to the viewer, where

Top: Most azaleas have numerous flowers and leaves that are smaller and more delicate than those of rhododendrons. Bottom: Look to larger rhododendrons like 'Hallelujah' to add a bold display to your landscape.

the full color and detail of individual specimens are best appreciated. But you can also use azaleas in highly formal ways. They can be severely pruned to create spheres that look like cushions of moss or to produce an aged, "oriental" effect.

Camellias can be used alone as specimen plants in a shady lawn area, but their sinuous branches encourage more sophisticated uses—as espaliers against a wall or as avenues or tunnels. They are cherished as greenhouse and conservatory plants more than any other genus, since they flower freely during the winter months, when few azaleas or rhododendrons are in bloom. In the middle of winter, when piles of snow blanket the ground, walking into a cool greenhouse and seeing camellias in full flower is an uplifting experience.

LEARNING ABOUT RHODO-DENDRONS AND AZALEAS

When the great plantsman Linnaeus started his famous classification of plants, he thought that rhododendrons and azaleas were in different plant genera; later botanical study proved beyond doubt that azaleas are really in the same genus, *Rhododendron*, as rhododendrons. Even though rhododendrons and azaleas are in the same genus, the gardening public and the nursery industry prefer to make a distinction. Here are some accepted differences between rhododendrons and azaleas.

Rhododendrons

•Leaves are usually large, broad, long, and leathery in texture.

•Flowers are usually large, and many are bell shaped.

•Flowers are borne in trusses at the ends of the branches.

•Flowers often have 10 or more stamens.

Azaleas

•Leaves are usually small, narrow, and pointed.

•The underside of a leaf usually has small hairs, especially along the midrib.

•Flowers are borne along the sides and on the tips of the stems.

•Flowers have five lobes to the flower.

•Flowers usually have five stamens.

Rhododendrons are generally more massive than azaleas. Their growth habit is more upright and is either bushy or treelike, although some are as small or smaller than evergreen azaleas. Although well-grown rhododendrons can make a spectacular display, they look best when given lots of room in an informal setting. Rhododendrons typically have sinuous branches with bold, boat-shaped leaves. The flowers are large and mostly borne in dome-shaped trusses.

Rhododendrons in the United States, especially in the Northeast and Northwest, are earning a worldwide reputation. The rhododendrons of Oregon and Washington can compete with the best the British have to offer.

In general, azaleas are short in stature, spreading and shrublike. They have brittle, twiggy branches with small, narrow leaves and large numbers of relatively small blossoms. Generally speaking, the more compact growth habit of azaleas adds to their versatility in the home landscape. Azaleas not only make beautiful specimen plants as a lawn centerpiece, for example, but also can be planted close together to form a mass planting or a dense flowering hedge. Azaleas will even grow contentedly in containers, and some azaleas make superb bonsai subjects. Some varieties can be severely pruned for use in highly formal gardens or left to grow uninhibited in natural, informal landscapes. They are also easy to work into tight spaces, and even the smallest garden or backyard can accommodate them.

With azaleas, it's easy to make a mass color statement. Some bloom so abundantly that the blossoms completely hide the foliage. You can blend several plants of different colors to create what appears to be a multicolored shrub.

The conditions in many parts of North America are ideal for growing azaleas. Many varieties of azaleas—notably the Southern Indian hybrids—do well in the South; others—such as the Kaempferi hybrids and deciduous azaleas—are sufficiently hardy to perform well in Maine and even Canada. Deciduous azaleas do very well in the Pacific Northwest, and most evergreen azaleas perform best where summers are humid.

RHODODENDRON AND AZALEA CLASSIFICATION

There are more than eight hundred species of plants in the genus *Rhododendron* and probably another eight thousand recognized hybrids. The hybrids are the results of elaborate cross-

Elepidote rhododendrons (top) lack scales and often have relatively large, broad leaves. Lepidote rhododendrons (bottom) have tiny dotlike scales on the undersides of their small, narrow leaves.

breeding not only between the species but also between hybrids and hybrids, and hybrids and species. The botanical classification of the genus is extremely complex and is constantly changing as research reveals new relationships between groups, and to accommodate the official rules of taxonomy.

Though the enthusiast need not understand the complexities of rhododendron taxonomy, the following groupings are useful to know.

- Lepidote rhododendrons
- Elepidote rhododendrons
- Evergreen azaleas
- Deciduous azaleas

Lepidote means scaly, and most small-leaved rhododendrons fit into this group. On the underside of a lepidote rhododendron leaf are the small scales, which resemble dots. The lepidote category comprises about five hundred wide-ranging species, about half of which are tropical (from Indonesia and Malaysia). Others in this group are tender epiphytes growing in the crotches of trees in humid rain forests, and some are hardy alpines.

Elepidote means without scales and describes rhododendrons that are evergreen and often broad-leaved. Elepidote rhododendrons are the rhododendrons typically grown in home gardens.

Azaleas are generally classified as evergreen or deciduous. Actually, evergreen types sometimes do lose some or all of their leaves in colder regions, so they are only semievergreen. Azaleas do not have scales like lepidote rhododendrons, but many have tiny hairs covering the leaf surface. The most popular evergreen azaleas include the Kurume hybrids; Kaempferi hybrids; Southern Indian hybrids; Gable hybrids; Glenn Dale hybrids; and many recently introduced hybrid groups, including the Back Acres, Girard, Harris, Linwood, North Tisbury, and Robin Hill azaleas. The most popular deciduous groups of azalea hybrids include the Exbury hybrids; Knap Hill hybrids; and the

Top: Azaleas need not be in mass plantings to be effective in a landscape. Light green leaves and the delicate features of these azalea flowers contribute to the tranquil mood of this small garden pond. Bottom: Tea is a camellia—(Camellia sinensis). Its similarity to ornamental camellias can be seen by looking at the leaves and flowers.

North American species, including *R. calendu-laceum* and *R. canadense*.

ABOUT CAMELLIAS

Although camellias resemble rhododendrons in some respects—in their leaf shapes, branch configurations, and cultural needs, for example—they are not closely related. Camellias belong to a distinctly different family of plants, the family *Theaceae,* of which the tea plant (*Camellia sinensis*) is commercially important.

Even if camellias never bloomed, their lovely, evergreen foliage would make them garden-worthy. The leaves are oval, pointed, and slightly toothed along the edges. They are everything a leaf should be—dark green on the top, light green on the underside, and usually glossy. They have substance, with the feel of polished leather. The lush, dark foliage is a perfect foil for the best feature of the camellia—its showy, solitary, rounded flowers. The flowers range from pristine white to all shades of pink to the deepest of reds, and many are variegated. The six standard terms used to describe the different forms of the blossoms are *single, semidouble, anemone, peony, rose form double,* and *formal double.*

The sinuous, gray branches of camellia plants are pliable and ideal for training against the side of a house to create espalier designs. The plants can also be pruned of their lower side branches to create beautiful "avenues" or "camellia tunnels."

As the camellia plants age, they tend to shed their lower branches, leaving a clump of sleek, upright main trunks with smooth, gray bark supporting a dense overhead canopy. In poor soils the trunks can become distorted, twisting and writhing to form impenetrable thickets. The trunks and branches may support vigorous populations of green algae, lichens, and epiphytic plants such as Spanish moss, heightening their aura of mystery.

Camellias usually flower between September and April (their bloom season is delayed in colder areas). They are sensitive to heavy frosts and freezing, which restrict their use as outdoor ornamental shrubs to the southeastern United States and the Pacific Coast. However, camellias require only frost exclusion to perform well and can be grown indoors, especially in greenhouses or sunrooms. Many miniature varieties have been developed to perform well as flower-

Flower Forms

Single ('Tanya')

Semidouble ('Lady Vansittart')

Peony ('Nuccio's Jewel')

Anemone ('Elegans')

Rose form double ('Elvige')

Formal double ('Mathotiana Alba')

ing houseplants, provided nighttime temperatures are about 45° F and the air is kept humid.

Even in mild-winter areas many gardeners prefer to grow camellias under glass. In areas where flowers and buds can be blemished by an unexpected frost, greenhouses are used to grow camellias. These are usually unheated structures attached to the house, and their sole purpose is to exclude frost.

There are about two hundred species of camellias, but three are of major importance to North American gardens: *Camellia japonica, C. sasanqua,* and *C. reticulata.*

Top: Camellia japonica
'Mrs. Tingley'.
Bottom left: Camellia
reticulata
'Captain Rawes'.
Bottom right: Camellia
sasanqua *'Yuletide'.*

Camellia japonica   Japonica, as it is commonly called, and its many cultivars are the most popular camellia species in cultivation. Over five thousand *C. japonica* cultivars are registered. It is a large shrub or small tree with glossy green leaves, and it usually has an upright habit. A very old plant may grow to 20 feet or more, but most mature varieties are between 8 and 10 feet high. Tall varieties may reach 12 to 15 feet. *C. japonica* varieties grow best in partial shade.

Camellia sasanqua   Next to the japonicas, the sasanquas are the most commonly grown camellias. The sasanqua camellias actually include varieties of three species: *Camellia sasanqua*, *C. hiemalis*, and *C. vernalis*. As a rule, the sasanquas are large shrubs or small trees with glossy leaves. Their growth habit is bushier than that of *C. japonica*, and the leaves are smaller. *C. sasanqua* is native to Kyushu, the southern island of Japan, and the Ryukyu Islands. The sasanquas are not as hardy as the *C. japonica* varieties, and their flowers are not as showy. But they bloom profusely, and are more sun tolerant than the japonicas.

Camellia reticulata   This is the third most popular camellia. It is a small to medium-sized tree native to southern China. The reticulatas have a more open and upright branching habit than the japonicas and sasanquas. Leaves are large, and dull rather than glossy. The flowers are quite large, up to 6½ inches or more in width, ranging from light pink to red.

HISTORY AND DEVELOPMENT

The most famous member of the camellia family is the tea plant (*C. sinensis*), vast plantations of which are concentrated in hilly regions of northern India, Sri Lanka (formerly Ceylon), and eastern China and Japan. All true camellias are evergreen and native to Asia.

Camellias have been popular for their ornamental value in Japanese and Chinese gardens for several thousand years; the first specimens to reach Europe arrived by ship from China in the 1730s. The first tea plant arrived in Europe in 1768. When specimens of the beautiful *C. japonica* 'Alba Plena' reached England aboard a ship of the East India Company in 1792, European gardeners clamored for more, and the popularity of camellias was assured. Even today, 'Alba Plena'—an early-flowering formal double, glistening white—is one of the most popular and widely available camellias.

As trade with Japan opened up, Europeans discovered more varieties of camellias. Many Europeans began hybridizing new cultivars or introducing Asian varieties under Westernized names. The name of a pink formal double Japanese variety, 'Usu-Otome', was changed to 'Pink Perfection' in order to help sell it in North America; German nurseries sold it as 'Frau Minna Seidel'.

The first camellia in North America—a single red *C. japonica*, came from England to Hoboken, New Jersey, about 1798. In 1800 'Alba Plena' was added to the plants at Hoboken. Soon camellias were the style for greenhouses in Boston and New York. From 1840 to 1850, Philadelphia became a center for camellia growing, and the Pennsylvania Horticultural Society and the Massachusetts Horticultural Society took the lead in popularizing the new flowering shrub.

Large outdoor collections soon became part of plantation life in the port cities of South Carolina, Alabama, Louisiana, and Mississippi. Camellias introduced to Middleton Place Plantation and Magnolia Gardens in the 1830s or 1840s are now mature, flowering trees. Hybrid camellias—like hybrid rhododendrons—are becoming more available as gardenworthy plants. The first hybridizing effort between two species was made by J. C. Williams, at Caerhays Castle in Cornwall, England. He also developed many famous rhododendron hybrids.

The finest of his camellias—crosses of *C. japonica* with *C. saluenensis*—are referred to as Williamsii hybrids.

Important camellia breeding is being done today in the United States as well as in Australia, New Zealand, Japan, China, England, and Europe.

In the future, exciting new colors are expected to appear—such as peach, apricot, and orange—through hybridizing with the newly obtained yellow *C. chrysantha*. Work is also progressing on hybridizing for more fragrant flowers, cold hardiness, and heat tolerance.

This classy camellia has had its lower branches pruned to form a stylish small tree.

Landscaping With Azaleas, Rhododendrons, and Camellias

Rhododendrons, azaleas, and camellias are surprisingly versatile as landscape plants.

As individual plants, rhododendrons, azaleas, and camellias are beautiful. But much of their beauty in the garden lies in how well they complement each other and the plantings around them. Even if you're just replacing a few plants, and most certainly if you're planting a new garden, carefully consider the effect of each plant's growth habit: mature height and spread, denseness or openness, and foliage texture. Be aware of the colors and textures of existing plants and take them into account when designing new plantings.

Rhododendrons, azaleas, and camellias range from tree to open shrubs to sprawling ground covers. Some of them grow slowly to their mature height. Others grow to a substantial size in only a few years. Take these factors into account when selecting plants. Some of the very tall rhododendrons are well suited to a natural landscape, such as the far side of a pond or lake. They can be used in a more formal manner to line a wide driveway. Ground-hugging, dwarf rhododendrons and azaleas are ideal for confined spaces, such as rock gardens. Some azaleas, such as the North Tisbury hybrids, have been developed as ground covers. Others—such as the Gable, Southern Indian, and Kaempferi hybrids—will form tall, dense, flowering hedges after 10 to 15 years. Camellias vary considerably in their habits, too. Some are upright and spreading and others are globose, or round. The sasanqua hybrids are

Rhododendrons, camellias, and azaleas can be used as specimen plants—as this rhododendron, 'Anah Kruschke', is being used—or as massed plantings or ground covers.

often compact and bushy, and some even grow low enough to make good ground covers.

The flowering times of rhododendrons, azaleas, and camellias vary considerably. For example, *Rhododendron schlippenbachii* (the royal azalea) blooms in the spring—in some locations right after the earliest daffodils. *R. prunifolium* (the plum-leaved azalea) blooms in midsummer. Camellias usually bloom during the winter and early spring months. *Camellia sasanqua,* however, blooms in the fall. Flowering times also vary from year to year, depending on the weather conditions. If you wish to make effective companion plantings, flowering times are especially important. For example, contrasting Spanish bluebells (*Endymion hispanicus*) with red azaleas requires precise selection of varieties so the two will reach peak bloom together. Likewise, if you'd like several varieties of rhododendrons to bloom simultaneously, you'll need to plan carefully.

An obvious but essential element in planning a garden is color. Do the bloom colors complement each other, or do they clash? How do nearby foliage colors interact with each other? A plant with blue-gray leaves is not likely to harmonize with a plant bearing yellow-green leaves. If you wish to emphasize a particular flower color, be aware of the foliage color around it. A corner planting of several strikingly variegated shrubs planted among several stoplight red azaleas will compete for visual attention, creating a busy look. One way to accommodate several different, potentially clashing color schemes is to select plants that bloom at different times.

LANDSCAPE USES

Some plants are useful in only a few landscape situations. Not so with camellias, azaleas, and rhododendrons. There is bound to be a species or hybrid just right to make just the

Simple yet spectacular, these azalea beds are composed of just three colors and one basic shape, yet they create a colorful and pleasing display.

right statement in any landscape—from a container planting to a woodland planting, from a bonsai to a hedge, or from a rock garden to a windbreak.

Beds and Borders

Beds and borders are two common locations for rhododendrons, azaleas, and camellias. Beds are islands of cultivated soil surrounded by lawn, flagstones, paving, or brick. They allow plants to be seen from all sides and can be square, round, or free-form. Borders are beds backed by a fence, wall, hedge, or line of trees. They are the most common ways to display azaleas, rhododendrons, and camellias in a home landscape. When designing beds and borders, allow for enough room between the plants so that the outline of each plant is clearly defined.

Island beds are usually the best places for sun-loving azaleas and rhododendrons. An island bed allows overall ventilation and lighting, which these plants need. Where some shade is necessary, borders may be a better choice, since the proximity of a background—such as the shady side of a house or overhanging trees—provides the necessary protection.

To prepare an island bed, pile the soil higher in the center. To prepare a border, pile the soil higher at the back. When using plants of different heights, be sure to plant them so tall varieties do not obscure smaller ones.

"Ring around a tree" is a popular form of island bed for azaleas, camellias, and dwarf rhododendrons. A tree with a single trunk and a spreading canopy, such as a redbud or a large flowering dogwood, is an ideal candidate for a circular bed. Improve the soil by working 2 inches of peat moss and an inch of aged compost into the top 6 inches of soil. Be careful not to disturb large plant roots. Since azaleas and camellias are not as competitive as lawn grass, a bed of this sort will actually benefit the tree.

In small gardens, camellias and azaleas are planted as specimens in mixed herbaceous borders or as foundation plantings. In these landscapes, camellias and azaleas are in close formation with other acid-loving plants, such as rhododendrons, andromeda, holly, gardenias, and nandina.

Camellias are favorite plants to train along the wall of a house or along a tall fence as an espalier. The taller varieties have pliable branches that can be bent and secured to the wall or fence to create parallel lines of color, or they can be spread out to create a fan effect.

Hedges, Screens, and Windbreaks

Shrubs planted close together create a solid wall of greenery. Depending on the height, this type of planting can be a hedge, screen, or windbreak. Hedges are often low and serve to delineate a garden space or to direct movement from one area to another. Formal hedges, used to create patterns, are severely pruned so the edges are clean and well-defined. Azaleas are excellent candidates for formal hedges.

Left: Rhododendrons make an easy-to-care-for informal screen. This one is 'Cornish Red'.
Right: A bed of Kurume azaleas under a cherry tree creates a Japanese ambience.

Top: Camellias make excellent hedges. Prune them right after flowering to avoid removing flower buds.
Bottom: A hillside planting of rhododendrons thrives in the shade.

Azaleas, rhododendrons, and camellias are all good candidates for informal hedges, which are left unpruned. Tall enough to hide unsightly views or provide a visual enclosure, screens create privacy in a yard or garden. Both rhododendrons and camellias can be planted as screens.

Rhododendrons by themselves are generally unsuitable as windbreaks, since they don't do well in exposed locations where they are subject to dry conditions. However, used in a double line with trees, rhododendrons make a windbreak that is also a beautiful landscape feature. The first line can be a tough conifer, such as a Norway Spruce or Scotch Pine, to break the initial force of the wind. The second line can be rhododendrons. The conifers form a perfect backdrop for the flowers.

Woodland Plantings

Azaleas and rhododendrons are indispensable for woodland gardens. Some of the finest woodland gardens in the world rely heavily on rhododendrons and azaleas for intense color. Camellias are used in these gardens to add color during the winter months. A wonderful companion plant for woodland azaleas is the flowering dogwood (particularly the white form), which blooms at the same time and contrasts effectively with the predominating pinks and reds of azaleas. The ideal woodland environment is one in which tall deciduous trees or tall open-crown evergreens have had their lower branches trimmed away, allowing free air movement and creating dappled shade.

The Oriental Landscape

Rhododendrons, camellias, and especially azaleas are ideal plants for Japanese- or Chinese-style gardens. *Rhododendron yakushimanum, R. kiusianum,* lepidote rhododendrons, and Satsuki azaleas are appropriate selections for an oriental garden. In an oriental landscape, the plants are often severely pruned to attain a specific shape. Where foliage color and shape are the desired goals, flowering characteristics are less important. The following three styles, oriental in their origin, adapt easily to a North American home landscape.

Natural   Plants are massed along a slope, beside a bridge or rustic building, or beside a lake; this helps create a natural, untamed look.

Sheared   Drastic shearing in the shape of a dome or pillow is the desired effect in this sort of landscape. The smooth mounds introduce a soft, tranquil mood to the landscape, as cushions of moss would do on a smaller scale. Heavy shearing of azaleas reduces the number of blossoms, since the shrubs usually need shearing twice a year to keep the contour smooth—in spring, immediately after the blossoms die, and again in late June to early July. Although the second shearing gives the azalea little time to produce new flower buds, it actually creates an attractive effect, since it encourages the emergence of rich green foliage shoots against which the few blossoms are highlighted like stars. Any late vegetative growth in the fall will be above the flowering shoots and can be cut back.

Artistically pruned   To create this type of landscape, the thicket of lower main branches is thinned out dramatically and the lower side branches are stripped away. A dense canopy of foliage, like an umbrella or mushroom, is allowed to form. The pruning emphasizes sinuous lines and creates the illusion of age and sculpturing by the elements—the kind of sculpturing that might happen over many years on an exposed cliff or mountaintop.

The Rock Garden

Since many species of azaleas and rhododendrons come from mountainous regions, a rock garden is a great place to display them. Create the rock garden along a sunny or partially shaded slope backed by tall evergreen rhododendrons or a windbreak of dense pines.

In a very formal way, a sheared azalea in a Japanese garden suggests a hill.

Creating a Bonsai

Azaleas, lepidote rhododendrons, and camellias make magnificent bonsai subjects. Bonsai is the art of pruning and shaping plants to dwarf them for display in special trays. Azaleas are particularly good subjects for creating bonsai masterpieces; most notable for this purpose are the species *Rhododendron kiusianum* and *R. serpyllifolium* and the Kurume and Satsuki hybrids. Camellias are also favorite bonsai subjects. Particularly appropriate for bonsai are *Camellia sasanqua* 'Yuletide', *C. hiemalis* 'Bonsai Baby', and *C. japonica* 'Higo'.

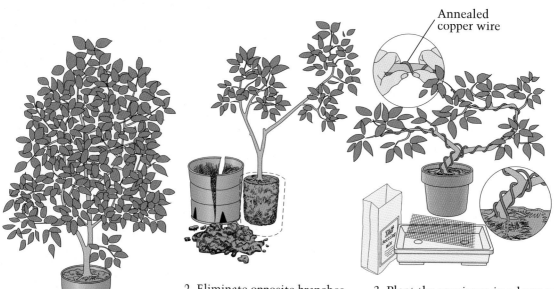

Annealed copper wire

1. Select a plant that suggests an interesting form.

2. Eliminate opposite branches and growth from the underside of branches. Cut back long branches to the size you want. Remove the rootball from the can, and cut it down by one third to one half without disturbing the roots near the trunk.

3. Plant the specimen in a large pot and shape it with wire. Anchor the wire in the soil and wrap it loosely around the trunk and main branches without scarring the bark. Bend gently, a little at a time with your thumbs opposite the wire to shape the plant. Make bends a little at a time every few weeks. After a year in the pot, put the plant into a permanent bonsai container.

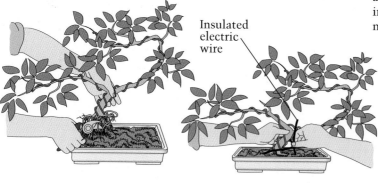

Insulated electric wire

4. A week or so before transplanting, prune back most of the new top growth so the plant is shaped just as you want it. Lift the plant from the pot, loosen the rootball, and cut away about one third of the roots. Don't cut the main horizontal roots or feeder roots near the surface. Keep the roots moist as you work.

5. Spread the roots evenly and position the plant in the container. Secure the plant with insulated electrical wire that runs through the drain holes and over the roots. Add potting mix to fill all the spaces between the roots with your fingers. Water thoroughly, then add a layer of pebbles or moss.

6. Your bonsai is ready to display. To maintain your bonsai, keep the container moist and pinch off new unwanted growth before it becomes woody.

The most beautiful rock gardens combine three elements: plants, rocks, and water—especially water that trickles over rocks and forms informal, naturalistic pools. Water is a very desirable feature near azaleas and rhododendrons. It not only helps create a cool, humid environment, it mirrors the flower display, doubling its color impact. Most rock gardens featuring rhododendrons will benefit from an underground watering system. Rhododendrons are adapted to high altitudes where they are constantly shrouded in mist; if subjected to desert-dry conditions for any length of time, they wilt and die. Though some tall and medium varieties can be planted as highlights, rock gardeners particularly favor azaleas and the dwarf alpine rhododendron species and hybrids. Plant these in deep pockets of leaf mold among the rocks.

Container Plantings

Many rhododendrons, azaleas, and camellias are especially suited to life in containers, whether in tubs on a patio or terrace, hanging baskets, or bonsai trays. In areas with alkaline or problem soils, growing these plants in containers makes especially good sense because it's easier to make a soil mix for a container than to amend unsuitable outdoor soil.

Many slow-growing dwarf varieties of rhododendrons and azaleas are eminently suitable for container growing, but some pinching and pruning may be necessary to maintain an attractive shape. See pages 32 and 33 for special tips on pruning. Just about any camellia can be grown in large containers, and many varieties have been developed especially for containers. Indeed, some are small and compact and can be grown as houseplants as long as the humidity is high. 'Nuccio's Gem' (white) and 'Nuccio's Cameo' (pink) are especially suitable as houseplants. Also, there are some compact forms of *Camellia sasanqua* that will grow indoors.

It is easier to grow plants in large containers, but the larger they are, the more difficult it is to move them. If container mobility is important, consider setting the pots on platforms with wheels. The plants can then be kept outdoors on a patio and easily wheeled under cover if a frost threatens at flowering time.

Except for bonsai subjects, a gallon-capacity container is the smallest to consider starting with. You can always transfer the plant to a larger container when the plant becomes rootbound. All containers should have adequate drainage holes. Place a plastic screen over the hole or holes, to prevent the soil from washing out. Certain varieties of azaleas are particularly effective in hanging baskets. Some of the Belgian and Satsuki hybrids—such as 'Flame Creeper' and 'Pink Cascade'—have a naturally spreading, pendulous habit that can make a beautiful basket without tedious training. The best hanging baskets consist of wire frames, in which moist sphagnum moss is packed around the sides to form a "nest" for the soil mix. Though camellias are difficult to cultivate in hanging baskets, some spreading and pendulous varieties of *Camellia sasanqua* and hybrids such as 'Tiny Princess' can be successful.

Camellias, azaleas, and rhododendrons all adapt well to container culture. Use a soil mix that is rich in peat moss (which is very acid) and a container with a capacity greater than 1 gallon.

Caring for Azaleas, Rhododendrons, and Camellias

The time and energy spent in preparing the site properly and taking care of their basic needs will pay off in plants that are healthy and beautiful.

Rhododendrons, azaleas, and camellias will mature into healthy, attractive plants, reliably blooming year after year, if given the proper growing conditions. Established, vigorous plants need a minimal amount of maintenance. Selecting the right varieties, preparing the site well, and meeting their basic care requirements will ensure success.

Before you begin planting azaleas, camellias, and rhododendrons, make sure that the varieties will perform well in your area and the precise location in which you wish to plant them. Whatever you do, don't just pop down to a local discount center and load up with some favorite colors on sale. Look for species or hybrid names and find out how the plants will perform.

Azaleas, camellias, and rhododendrons grow well in many areas of North America. They do exceptionally well in areas close to oceans or other great bodies of water, such as the Great Lakes. In the Deep South, azaleas do better than rhododendrons except for the newer tropical rhododendrons from Indonesia and Malaysia.

As you can see by checking the distribution maps in the encyclopedia section, different varieties and groups of rhododendrons, azaleas, and camellias do well in different areas. For example, the Southern Indian azaleas are not reliably hardy north of Washington, D.C.; the Belgian Indians do better in southern California and the lower South; the Glenn Dale hybrids are hardy, but the Gable hybrids are hardier still. The Kaempferi hybrids are hardier than the Kurumes.

Given shade, moisture, and acid soil, azaleas like this 'Hinode Giri' thrive with little care.

Look for named varieties free of diseases and pests when buying balled-and-burlapped plants.

check them carefully. The foliage should be healthy; avoid plants with yellowing or spotted leaves. Inspect the stems and the upper and lower surfaces of leaves for diseases and insects. Plants sold at a garden center are usually in containers, or the rootball may be wrapped in burlap or plastic, which is gathered around the stem with string or a plastic tie. The best time to buy plants is when they are in bloom so you can see what color and size the blossoms actually are. If there is any delay between buying plants and planting, do not leave the plants exposed to full sun. Give them shade and water them regularly until you can place them in their permanent positions.

SELECT A SITE

All things considered, rhododendrons, azaleas, and camellias are relatively easy plants to grow. But there are some important factors to be considered when deciding where to plant them in your garden or yard. Pay particular attention to soil, light, and, in cold areas, winter protection.

Soil and Drainage

Rhododendrons, azaleas, and camellias prefer well-drained soils. If you're not sure how well your soil drains, dig a hole about a foot deep and fill it with water. Let it drain, and fill it again. If the water stays at the same level for several hours the second time, your soil has poor drainage.

Improve drainage by creating raised beds or a mound with coarse pine or fir bark, coarse sawdust, or other organic materials. Use raw bark and coarse sawdust from logging mills rather than fine sawdust from building material outlets. The remedy for soils that do not retain water is to add lots of organic material, such as leaf mold, pine bark, coarse peat moss, or compost. The organic material adds moisture-holding ability to sandy soil. In the case of clay, it breaks up the tightly arranged soil particles, introducing air spaces.

Avoid placing foundation plantings adjacent to concrete or gravel paths containing alkaline minerals, such as landscape chips or oyster shells. Leaching of minerals from a wall or path can stunt growth and even kill a plant unless you treat the soil as the following paragraph describes.

A good pH range for rhododendrons, azaleas, and camellias is 5 to 6. Wherever the soil

Light shade suits all camellia varieties, but those of *Camellia sasanqua* can usually tolerate more sun than other varieties, especially in hot, dry climates. In climates where humidity is high—such as the Pacific Northwest—camellias can tolerate more sun than in climates that are hot and dry. Even in more humid climates, white and pale pink blossoms may burn if exposed to direct sun. Only the darker colors should receive any direct sun.

Generally speaking, camellias do well in areas where winter temperatures do not fall below 5° F. In terms of plant hardiness, *C. japonica* is the most hardy, *C. sasanqua* is next, and *C. reticulata* the least hardy. Since many camellias require little more than frost exclusion, they can be grown under glass with minimum winter protection.

The first question when buying plants is whether to use young and yearling stock or to pay the extra price for mature container-grown or balled-and-burlapped plants. Yearling stock and container-grown or balled-and-burlapped plants are most readily available from local sources. Very young plants are generally supplied by mail-order specialists. Buying young plants makes sense when you intend to create a large mass planting and wish to economize. Usually, it is best to acclimatize the small plants by setting them in temporary beds under shade until they have grown to blooming size and then move them to permanent quarters.

Plants sold at garden centers are almost always blooming size. When selecting plants,

is too alkaline, modify the backfill soil with 50 percent peat moss to reduce the pH and provide organic matter. For established plants in alkaline soil, treat the soil with ferrous sulfate, ammonium sulfate, or sulfur. Follow label directions when using chemical additives to prevent toxicity problems in the soil with repeated use. Follow this treatment with a mulch of shredded peat moss or pine needles. To keep the soil from becoming alkaline again, fertilize with ammonium sulfate or other acid-forming fertilizers.

If you are in any doubt about the acidity of your soil, send a sample to a soil-testing laboratory. Contact your local extension service for information. Except in California and Illinois, state universities provide soil tests at modest cost, giving precise recommendations for amending soil to grow specific plants. In California and Illinois, the extension service will provide a list of commercial soil-testing laboratories. For more on amending alkaline soil, see page 45.

Sun or Shade

Generally speaking, azaleas tolerate a greater light intensity than camellias or rhododendrons, except for certain alpine rhododendron varieties that demand full sun. Though both rhododendrons and azaleas tolerate full sun, over most of North America a lightly shaded site is preferable. In light shade the plants are less susceptible to dehydration, and flowers retain their color better. Camellias are much less

sun tolerant than azaleas and rhododendrons. Avoid planting camellias near highly reflective walls—such as light-colored stucco or white-washed fences—unless these surfaces are shaded or are along the north side of a building.

In areas where moisture is abundant and nights are cool, sun or shade isn't a critical choice. But in most areas, where summer droughts are common, an open, sunny location could be lethal unless the soil is adequately watered. Light shade or filtered sunlight is best. In dense shade plants become spindly and may not form flower buds. If dense shade is cast by low-growing evergreens or deciduous trees, increase the light intensity by pruning overhanging limbs. The pruning of a single branch can make a measurable difference in

Top: Hillsides are often ideal sites for rhododendrons and azaleas because sloping soil drains well.
Bottom: Most camellias, azaleas, and rhododendrons grow best in partial shade. A lathhouse provides an ideal growing site in a hot climate.

flowering performance of plants in densely shaded sites.

Protection From Wind and Cold

Avoid sites exposed to cold or constant winds—especially with rhododendrons and camellias. Where possible, place plantings away from prevailing winds (which blow west to east over most inland areas of North America). Good windbreaks can be made with high hedges of bushy shrubs or a line of coniferous evergreens. Generally speaking, walls and wooden fences by themselves are not always adequate since wind can hit a solid barrier with great force and jump right over it with equal velocity; a row of trees absorbs the wind and weakens it.

Shelter is especially important when plants are at the extreme limits of their hardiness zone. A plant that is recommended for Maine or Canada and is hardy to –25° F might easily freeze at a much higher temperature in an exposed situation. Shelter is also important on eastern or southern exposures in cold areas. Alternate thawing and freezing from bright winter sun can cause injury.

Avoid frost pockets; it's better to plant on a slope than at the lowest level, where cold air settles.

PLANTING AND CARE

Once you've prepared the site and selected the plants, much of the work is done. Planting them properly will get them off to a good start, and routine maintenance will help them stay healthy and beautiful.

Plant Installation

After you've provided proper drainage and amended the soil (see page 26), you're ready to plant. If you intend to install a mass planting, be sure to amend the entire area, rather than just the immediate area around each plant.

To plant each shrub, dig a hole 1 to 2 feet wider than the rootball. Leave the soil in the center of the hole undisturbed to prevent later settling of the plant. Mix in generous amounts of peat moss or other organic material to the soil removed from the hole (it should be at least a half soil, half amendment mix). Place the ball on the undisturbed soil, with the top slightly above the soil level. More rhododendrons, azaleas, and camellias die from being planted too deep than from all other causes. Fill the space around the sides with the amended soil mixture until the hole is about half full, and fill with water. Then, fill up the hole completely and water it again. This will settle the soil as well as water it.

A fence protects 'Bow Bells' rhododendrons from wind and full sun.

Planting

1. Dig the hole one or two feet wider than the rootball. Add organic matter to the soil removed from the hole.

Undisturbed soil

2. Remove the wrapping completely from the rootball. Center the rootball on the column of soil so the top is a little above grade. Back-fill about halfway and water to settle the soil.

Mulch

Basin berm

Rootball

3. Finish back-filling the hole so some of the rootball is showing. Make a watering basin a little larger than the rootball. Make certain the floor of the basin is level with the original grade. Soak thoroughly by filling the basin, then fill the basin with mulch.

Build a water basin around the plant with extra backfill soil or soil from outside the basin. Make sure the surface of the basin is level with the surrounding surface. Finally, cover the site with a nonfloating mulch to discourage weed growth.

Rhododendrons, azaleas, and camellias in containers or wrapped in burlap can be planted almost any time of year—even in full flower. The exceptions are extremely dry, hot, or cold periods. Fertilizer is useful during the first year even in good soils. Sprinkle a light application of fertilizer designed for rhododendrons, azaleas, and camellias (see the opposite page for more about fertilizers) around the drip line. However, don't fertilize plants in the late summer or fall—the tender growth that may result will be susceptible to winter damage in areas subject to freezing temperatures and conditions favoring desiccation.

Mulch around each plant with pine needles, aged wood chips, pine bark, or other decorative organic material to help conserve moisture, keep the soil cool, and control weeds.

Container-grown plants are the easiest to transplant. Turn the plant upside down and tap the container edge on a hard surface to loosen the plant. If the container is large, lay it on its side and tap the rim sharply with a hammer; the plant will slide out easily with its soil and roots intact. Plastic containers can easily be slid off the rootball. If the roots are growing out of the drainage holes, they may need to be trimmed before the plant can be removed from the container. After removing the rootball from a container, score the sides with a knife in several places; this will stimulate new root growth into the surrounding soil. If the plant is rootbound, remove an inch of soil and roots from the sides and bottom of the rootball. Slash the rootball at the base and the sides and pull the roots apart to loosen them.

Balled-and-burlapped plants—especially camellias—need more careful handling because the soil around the roots can crumble away when the burlap is removed. They also tend to be dry and in need of watering at the time of purchase, so before planting soak the rootball in water for at least 10 minutes (or an hour if the soil is extremely dry) or until the bubbles stop rising. The burlap does not always have to be removed. If the rootball will stay in one piece, go ahead and remove the burlap; if not, keep the burlap wrapped around the bottom and sides but open at the top. Just cut the string from around the stem to free the folds, and plant the rootball with the burlap in place; the burlap will decompose when covered with soil. However, if the burlap has been treated (usually dyed green) or if it is plastic, be sure to remove it. Balled-and-burlapped plants are often sold in fiber containers with the burlap still on the rootball. The fiber container can be planted, but it should be slashed in several places to hasten decomposition. The rim should also be torn off so it doesn't show. Make sure the burlap is untied from the trunk before planting. If you leave burlap in place around the rootball, make certain that none of it is above the surface of the ground. Exposed burlap can act like a wick, drawing water away from the roots as it evaporates from the exposed burlap.

Water

Water is the key to the growth of rhododendrons, azaleas, and camellias and must be supplied to the plants on a regular basis. During rainy seasons—such as winter and spring in the Pacific Northwest—the plants receive sufficient moisture on their own. Unfortunately, much of North America is subject to extremes of drought in summer and cold in winter. If a dry summer is followed by a hard winter, plant losses can be severe. A partially dehydrated plant that faces a cold, blustery winter has little chance of survival. If it does survive such stress, flowering will be sparse. Plant roots should be moist but not waterlogged. In the absence of natural rainfall, water is especially important during certain periods.

•Immediately after planting

•After flowering during summer, when new leaves and flower buds are forming

•In fall, prior to winter dormancy (to help the plant survive dehydration from winter winds)

•Any period of a week to 10 days without at least 1 inch of rain

The problem when watering is supplying enough to do the job. Standing around with a garden hose may save young annual plants, but it always seems as though you are supplying more water than you really are. Lawn sprinklers set into the middle of an azalea, camellia, or rhododendron bed are better because a sprinkler can be left for extended periods of time to give the soil a thorough soaking. But even sprinklers may have a hard time covering large plantings during a savage heat wave.

Another method is a drip irrigation system, which supplies water directly to the root zone. At the turn of a faucet, water drips from emitters or oozes from pores in the hose wall, thoroughly soaking the soil without wasting a drop. A drip irrigation system is easiest to install when a garden is being built. Such a system is more difficult to install in established gardens, especially in a mass planting. If your plants are established, cover the hoses with mulch to conceal them and prevent evaporation. If the water source contains sand or minerals, the small holes in the system can become clogged with mineral deposits after two or three years. Use a filter at the faucet connection to keep your drip system effective.

One method to increase humidity is to install an overhead mist system. The mist heads can be attached to the plants; tie the small hoses to the branches and stems. When installing either a drip irrigation system or a mist system in your garden, consider adding an automatic timing device to the system. These devices make watering effortless and ensure that sufficient water goes to each plant on a regular basis even when you're away.

Weeds

The less competition from other plants, the better your plants will grow. Weeds not only compete for moisture and nutrients, but also block out sunlight and reduce air circulation. Poison ivy or oak, wild grape, blackberries, and other aggressive woodland vines are particularly troublesome. To eliminate them they should be "grubbed" from the soil—dug up by the roots. But be careful weeding close to camellias, rhododendrons, or azaleas: Their fibrous root systems lie just beneath the surface and can be damaged by cultivators. Pull weeds by hand if possible.

Mulch

A mulch is any kind of soil covering. Mulches are vital for camellias, rhododendrons, and azaleas because these plants are shallow rooted. Mulch keeps the soil moist, friable, and cool at the soil surface, where the roots are. Unmulched soil packs down, has high daytime temperatures, and dries out frequently.

From 2 to 4 inches of organic mulch is the depth most effective for rhododendrons, azaleas, and camellias.

Fertilizers

Most rhododendrons, azaleas, and camellias are slow growers and light feeders. However, regular feedings of fertilizer will ensure vigorous growth and quality blooms. Two basic forms of fertilizers are available: organic and chemical. Organic fertilizers, such as fish emulsion, vary in their analysis or content of nutrients. However, they seldom burn the plants or cause salt buildup in the soil. The nutrients in chemical fertilizers are much more readily accessible to plant roots and are available in a wide range of concentrations. They are more quickly leached from the soil than organic fertilizers, however, and must be replaced more frequently.

For rhododendrons and azaleas If the soil around rhododendrons and azaleas is topped each season with several inches of compost or leaf mold, fertilizing is rarely necessary. If the soil is acid, plants are extremely efficient at extracting their own nutrients from these natural sources. However, since many soils are less than ideal and supplies of compost or leaf mold are not always available, a fertilizing schedule

Place 2 to 4 inches of organic mulch— such as pine needles, peat moss, or ground bark—around each rhododendron, azalea, and camellia plant to keep the soil moist, friable, and cool.

is often desirable. Feeding of azaleas should be restricted to the months of February to mid-April, particularly where winters are severe. Special fertilizers formulated for rhododendrons and azaleas may contain 10 percent nitrogen, 7 percent phosphorus, 7 percent potassium (10-7-7) or a similar formula. They may also contain three important trace elements: chelated iron, copper, and zinc.

Pruning Elepidote Rhododendrons

Head back elepidote rhododendrons by pruning just above any leaf whorl or where the scars show a leaf whorl was—any of the places marked here

Pruning Azaleas and Lepidote Rhododendrons

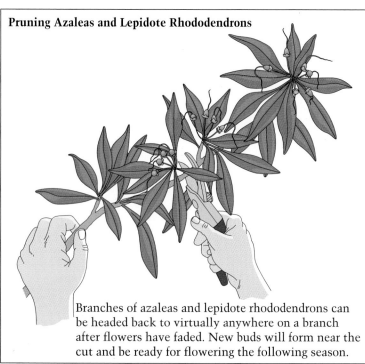

Branches of azaleas and lepidote rhododendrons can be headed back to virtually anywhere on a branch after flowers have faded. New buds will form near the cut and be ready for flowering the following season.

For camellias   The camellia is a strong feeder that does best with uniform moisture and a properly balanced fertilizer with 10 percent nitrogen, 7 percent phosphorus, and 7 percent potassium (10-7-7). Fertilizer of any type should be cast on the soil around the plant, starting halfway between the trunk and drip line and extending 6 to 12 inches beyond the drip line. It should be watered in well.

The basic feeding schedule consists of two to three feedings. Make the first application in March, before spring growth occurs. The second application should be in June, about the time flower buds are beginning to form. Apply the third in September to encourage better bloom color. A special camellia fertilizer (10-7-7) is preferable for the first two feedings, although a regular garden fertilizer (10-10-10) is acceptable. The fertilizer used in September should be low in nitrogen (0-10-10) to discourage any further leaf growth. In good soil, one feeding a year in the spring may be adequate. Follow label directions for the amount of fertilizer to apply.

Pruning

The need and technique for pruning depends on several factors, including the type of plant (azalea, rhododendron, or camellia) and the effect desired (shaping, thinning, or training).

For rhododendrons and azaleas   Azaleas and lepidote rhododendrons can be pruned hard virtually anywhere along a shoot. In a short time buds will appear to form new shoots capable of flowering the following season, especially if the pruning is done soon after spring flowering. Some cultivars of elepidote rhododendrons—the broad-leaved rhododendrons—may lose a season's bloom if pruned below the first set of leaves. Branches cut back too severely may not form side shoots. A good rule of thumb is to cut back one third of the plant. Evergreen azaleas require only light annual pruning in the majority of gardens. This is best done by using a pair of hand pruners or lopping shears to cut back branches right after the flowers have died, which gives the plants time to set new flower buds.

Late summer and fall pruning normally reduces the flower display the following year, except in areas that have a mild climate. Another way of pruning azaleas—called sculpture pruning—is popular in oriental gardens. To produce an interesting form and create the illusion of old age, remove carefully selected branches to open the canopy and display the remaining branches and trunk. Rhododendrons (and deciduous azaleas) should never be sheared like an evergreen azalea, since most gardenworthy rhododendrons are elepidotes, which need the most recent year's growth to produce flower buds. Simply thin out excessive branches or judiciously prune wayward branches to maintain a compact shape. Always prune above a rosette of leaves. Use a good hand pruner, never a hedge trimmer. You may need a tree saw to thin out really thick stems of rhododendrons. To encourage rhododendrons to branch sideways and form a more dense plant, freely pinch out terminal vegetative buds. This is most important on young, nonflowering plants. The form of most ungainly rhododendrons can be improved by heavy pruning done in stages over a period of two to three years.

For camellias Pruning camellias is not a common practice. Until fairly recently, it was not considered important to prune camellias, and plants were generally just allowed to grow. Pruning camellias, however, can benefit both the plant and the flowers.

The best camellia blooms are usually produced on vigorous plants, small to medium in size. As the plants grow, there are more growing points, and a larger number of flower buds are set per plant. The amount of shoot growth is reduced, and the individual flowers tend to be smaller.

Pruning of camellias should be done after blooming and before new growth begins. A pocket knife, pruning shears, and a small pruning saw are essential tools. After pruning, paint the cuts with pruning paint or some other protective material.

To prune properly, make the cut next to the trunk and do not leave stubs. Remove twigs that have only one weak terminal bud and no side buds. Vigorous shoots will have one to three well-developed terminal leaf buds and side buds as well. As a general rule, cut out branches that tend to grow inward, for they will certainly be shaded out in later years. Remove all dead and dying twigs.

Drastic pruning may be necessary to restore an old camellia to vigorous growth or to reduce

Sculpture Pruning

Prune lower foliage away and then "sculpt" the framework of the branches to give the azalea an oriental or bonsai look

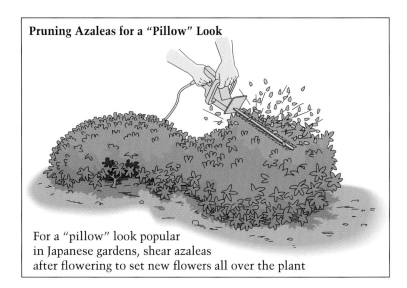

Pruning Azaleas for a "Pillow" Look

For a "pillow" look popular in Japanese gardens, shear azaleas after flowering to set new flowers all over the plant

it to a manageable size. To prune an old camellia, cut back each branch to a vigorous shoot, leaving it to grow. If no good shoots can be found, remove a large portion of the poorer branches, and wait to see which parts put out new growth.

Dead-Heading and Grooming

After a plant has flowered, it puts a lot of energy into forming seeds. Removal of the spent flowers before they have a chance to go to seed is called dead-heading, and it is a recommended practice to ensure bountiful floral displays from year to year. Unfortunately, dead-heading is impractical with most azaleas and many rhododendrons because the heads are much too numerous and too small. With the large-flowered rhododendrons, however, the procedure is quite simple: Pinch the flower head at a point where the brittle flower stem is attached to the main woody stem section. The flower head will snap away easily, but take care not to

Dead-heading

Remove spent flower heads where the brittle flower stem is attached to a main, woody stem by bending gently between your thumb and forefinger. Be careful not to damage the new buds.

Disbudding

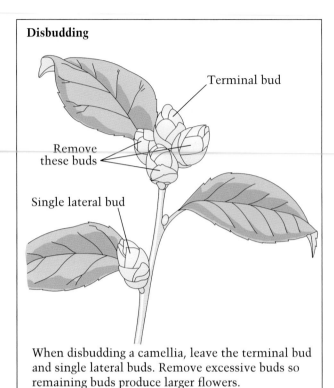

Terminal bud

Remove these buds

Single lateral bud

When disbudding a camellia, leave the terminal bud and single lateral buds. Remove excessive buds so remaining buds produce larger flowers.

Gibbing

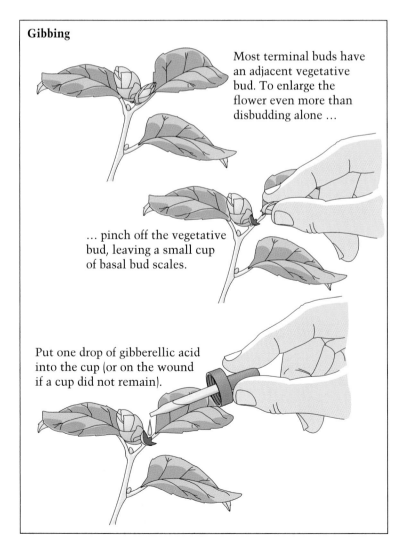

Most terminal buds have an adjacent vegetative bud. To enlarge the flower even more than disbudding alone ...

... pinch off the vegetative bud, leaving a small cup of basal bud scales.

Put one drop of gibberellic acid into the cup (or on the wound if a cup did not remain).

damage any small buds that have formed on either side of the flower stem, as you may damage part of next year's growth.

Disbudding and Gibbing

Two techniques used to improve the performance of camellias are disbudding and gibbing. Disbudding is the removal of excessive numbers of flower buds in the fall to allow the largest buds—usually the terminal buds—an opportunity to grow to a large size. Plants grown under glass or in the house are the most likely to be disbudded; those growing outdoors are generally left to set all of their flower buds.

Gibbing—the practice of applying a plant hormone, gibberellic acid—can be even more effective than disbudding in regard to increasing the size of blooms. Gibberellic acid is available from some nurseries, camellia mail-order sources, or the American Camellia Society (see address on page 92). Mix 1 gram of powdered gibberellic acid with 2 ounces of distilled water and apply to plants in late summer. Apply by pinching off a growth bud below a flower bud and using an eye dropper to place a drop of the solution on the wound. The larger the bush, the more buds you can treat. Most people like to leave about 80 percent untreated. Not all cultivars respond favorably to gibbing, but most of the common cultivars of *C. japonica* and

C. reticulata do, particularly two- to four-year-old plants. Gibbing in late summer and early fall produces early flowering and may change the shape and color of flowers. It is most successful if only a year or two of gibbing is followed by a year without gibbing.

Winter Protection

There are two basic approaches to winter survival of rhododendrons, azaleas, and camellias. You can select plants that can withstand the likely minimum temperature. Or you can provide physical barriers to insulate the plants from winter conditions. The encyclopedia section beginning on page 47 provides information on plant hardiness for a particular species or hybrid. However, at times even cold-hardy plants need additional protection to survive unusually severe winters.

For rhododendrons and azaleas Many species and varieties of azaleas and rhododendrons are among the hardiest of plants, and damage is usually not caused by low temperatures alone. Once frozen, a cold-hardy plant can remain safely dormant until it thaws during the warm days of spring. The trick is to keep it frozen and not subject it to repeated freezing and thawing. This is one of the reasons a sheltered, shaded area suits these plants well. In exposed situations wait until the ground freezes, then place a thick mulch around the plants. This will help keep the ground frozen until the real spring thaw occurs.

Although rhododendron branches are pliable and will bend under the weight of snow, certain domed-shaped or compact hybrids can suffer damage from heavy snowfalls or accumulations of ice, especially when they are sited under the eaves of a house. To protect these specimens, remove snow with a broom or consider placing a wooden frame over them.

Rhododendrons are especially susceptible to dehydration during their first two years in the garden, particularly if they are placed in exposed positions. In addition to watering well in the fall, you may want to erect a temporary windbreak using burlap sacking around a wooden frame.

For camellias Winter protection for camellias should fulfill several basic requirements.

Winter Protection

Wrap spongy plastic around the plant, and hold it in place with clothes pins

Top held with clothes pins

Round lid held on with clothes pins

"Tomato-cage" wire fencing protects spongy plastic

Small plants can be protected with cones of plastic and clothes pins anchored with rocks

Wire in the ground anchors the cage

•It should shield the plant from winter winds and severe temperature changes.

•Covers should be anchored so they do not blow off in strong winds.

•Protection should be structurally sound so it does not collapse under heavy snow.

Various methods and techniques may be used to meet these requirements. They generally involve some kind of support (stakes, poles, or sturdy wire) and a covering material (burlap, heavy blanket, or spongy plastic). The use of spongy plastic is relatively new but has produced excellent results even during abnormally cold winters. It is susceptible to deterioration from ultraviolet radiation, however, so an additional white plastic covering is advisable for plants in full sun.

PROPAGATION

Rhododendrons, azaleas, and camellias can be propagated by seed, stem cuttings, and layering. Camellias are also propagated by grafting.

Rhododendrons and Azaleas

The propagation methods described in this section are within the capability of typical home gardeners.

Seed Rhododendrons and azaleas set large numbers of very small, brown, winged or wingless seeds. The seeds ripen in autumn, and the elongated, cone-shaped brown pods turn brittle and split open.

Use seeds from hand-pollinated species or hybrids. Open pollinated hybrids will not produce seedlings that are true to the parent plant. Thus, seed collected from the hybrid 'Nova Zembla', for example, will not produce identical seedlings or flowering plants of 'Nova Zembla'.

Start the seed in flats, under shade, with a potting soil containing 2 parts peat moss (moisten thoroughly, then squeeze dry) and 1 part perlite. The fresher the seed, the better; no winter chilling is needed to break dormancy. Sprinkle seeds onto the surface, and keep the shredded sphagnum damp but not drenched. Cover the tray with glass or clear plastic to maintain high humidity. Germination takes up to four weeks at a soil temperature of 65° to 70° F.

After the seedlings have formed a true set of leaves, they can be transplanted to pots and placed outdoors in light shade. If there is danger of frost, keep them indoors or place them

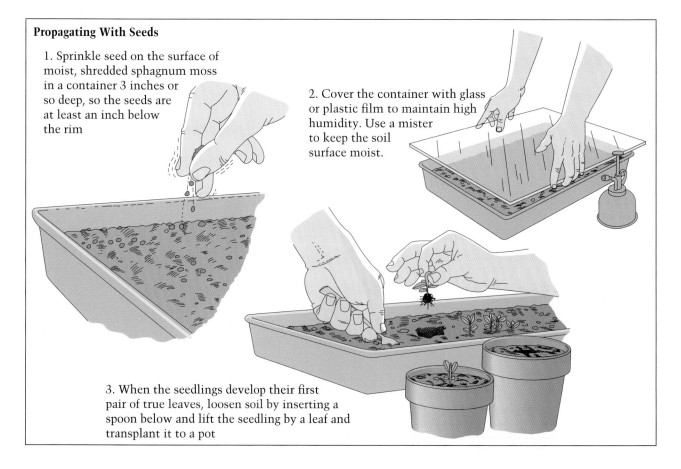

Propagating With Seeds

1. Sprinkle seed on the surface of moist, shredded sphagnum moss in a container 3 inches or so deep, so the seeds are at least an inch below the rim

2. Cover the container with glass or plastic film to maintain high humidity. Use a mister to keep the soil surface moist.

3. When the seedlings develop their first pair of true leaves, loosen soil by inserting a spoon below and lift the seedling by a leaf and transplant it to a pot

Propagating a Rhododendron From Cuttings

To propagate a rhododendron, select a new stem that is firm but just pliable so it will bend (top left). In general, about 30 days after flowering is a good time to take cuttings. Cut the stem so it is 3 to 5 inches long (top right). Remove the lower leaves (middle left). Cut the tops off the remaining leaves and make a lengthwise slice with a knife or razor blade at the base of the cutting to expose the inner wood (middle right). Dip the base of the stem into a rooting hormone (bottom left), then push the stem into the potting mix containing equal parts clean sand, peat, and fine pine bark or perlite (bottom right).

in cold frames. Use a potting soil of equal parts peat, fine pine bark, and perlite. Coarse sharp sand can also be added. Keep the soil mix moist and feed every two to four weeks with a dilute liquid fertilizer. When plants are 6 inches high, you can move them to permanent locations or set them into temporary nursery beds, under shade, for additional strengthening. If set out early enough, they will survive the winter in protected beds. Later seedlings should overwinter in a cold frame the first year.

Depending on the species or variety, rhododendrons may take from 3 to 10 years to flower when grown from seed. However, growing from seed is the most economical method of producing large quantities of seedlings.

Cuttings   Propagating plants from cuttings produces plants that are identical to the mother plant. Most of the native, deciduous azaleas are difficult to grow from cuttings. Take cuttings from deciduous azaleas early to get some growth started before fall, so the plants will survive the winter. You can take cuttings of rhododendrons and evergreen azaleas any time the plant is in active growth and when new growth becomes firm. As a general guide, 30 days after flowering is a good time to take cuttings.

Use a starter mix containing equal parts clean sand, peat, and fine pine bark (or perlite if pine bark is not available in your area). Take cuttings 3 to 5 inches long from the plant's outer areas of growth. Remove the lower leaves and, with a knife or razor blade, make a lengthwise cut (about ½ inch long) at the base of each cutting. The cut should be just deep enough to expose the inner wood.

Dip the base of each cutting into a rooting hormone, then push the cutting into the starter mix up to half its length. Lightly shade the cuttings and keep them moist in a tent of clear plastic. Cuttings should be well rooted within six weeks. After they have formed a healthy root system, transplant the cuttings to a pot or directly to a shaded outdoor location. Make sure that the soil is high in organic matter. It's better, although not always possible, to accomplish rooting and foliage growth in the same season than to try to nurse partly rooted stock through the winter. Overwinter any newly rooted cuttings in a cold frame.

Layering   The pliable branches of rhododendrons can easily be propagated by layering. Some lower, prostrate azaleas—with their shorter, erect branches—are not so easily propagated this way. Like cuttings, plants produced from layering are identical to the parent, but the procedure for obtaining large numbers of plants for mass plantings is more tedious.

Layering often occurs in nature when a branch arches down and touches moist soil. At the point of contact with the ground it produces roots and foliage. To propagate rhododendrons by layering, bend a branch down to the ground. At the point where it touches the soil, scratch or cut the bark (away from the parent plant) on the underside of the branch to speed the rooting process, then bury it 3 to 4 inches deep. Pin it to the soil with a forked stick or bent wire and cover the secured portion with a layer of peat moss or leaf mold to keep the branch from drying out. Keep the soil moist. After the branch has rooted (usually within a year), prune it from the parent and transfer it to a temporary shaded nursery bed to stimulate vigorous growth before transferring it to a permanent location.

Camellias

Like azaleas and rhododendrons, camellia plants can be propagated by several techniques, including seeds, cuttings, and layering. Grafting, however, is more commonly used than layering when propagating camellias.

Seed   Camellia seeds ripen in fall and are ½ inch or larger in size. Often there are two or three seeds inside the thick bushy seed capsule. Camellia seeds require temperatures between 70° and 85° F for germination. The seed coat is hard, so facilitate moisture penetration by filing the seed coat a bit with a nail file, or by nicking it with a sharp blade. Germination can be hastened by pouring boiling water over the seeds and allowing them to remain in the water for 24 hours. Plant the seeds about ¾ to 1 inch deep in a moist mixture composed of equal parts sand and peat moss. Germination takes three weeks or more. As the seed germinates, it will produce a long taproot. Gently lift the seedling from the soil and pinch off the root tip, then carefully replant the seedling. Pinching the main taproot will produce side

Layering

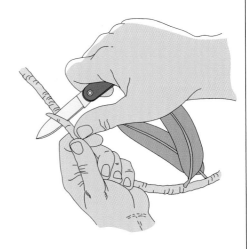

1. Select a branch that you can easily bend to the ground. Strip all leaves and shoots from about 4 inches to about 18 inches from the tip.

2. Scrape or cut some bark from the underside of the branch where it will contact the soil

3. Bury the branch so the tip will be about 6 to 8 inches out of the ground. Hold it with a stone or forked stick to keep it in place, if necessary.

4. When the branch has rooted and shows new growth (about one year), cut it from the parent plant

5. When roots are well developed, transplant the plant to a shaded nursery bed, and when well established, to its permanent place

Nurse Seed Grafting

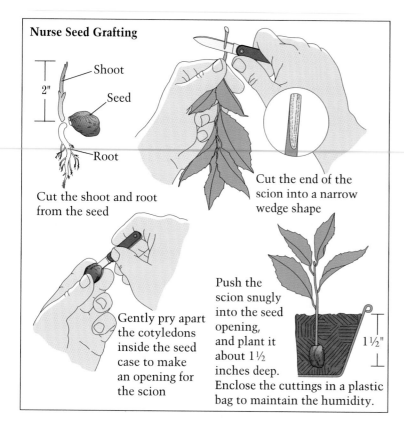

2"

Shoot

Seed

Root

Cut the shoot and root from the seed

Cut the end of the scion into a narrow wedge shape

Gently pry apart the cotyledons inside the seed case to make an opening for the scion

Push the scion snugly into the seed opening, and plant it about 1½ inches deep. Enclose the cuttings in a plastic bag to maintain the humidity.

1½"

Grafting

1. Cut off the camellia you plan on using as a rootstock 2 to 6 inches above the soil. A diamond cut with a flat top will aid in quick callusing.

Scion

Rootstock

2. Taper the scion so it has a ¾- to 1-inch wedge shape. Then split the rootstock to insert the scion.

3. Insert the scion so the thin, dark green cambium layer touches the cambium of the rootstock. Bind it with grafting tape or a rubber band.

roots, resulting in a bushier root system that's easier to transplant. Camellia plants grown from seeds will produce flowers in three years or more.

Camellias grown from seeds will vary from the parent. Propagation by cuttings, layering, or grafting will produce plants that are identical to the parent.

Cuttings   Camellia cuttings (or scions) should be 3 to 4 inches long. The procedure for rooting camellia cuttings is very similar to that of rooting azaleas and rhododendrons (see pages 37 and 38). However, there is an alternate method, called nurse seed grafting, that is usually more successful. This requires a newly germinated camellia seed. Use a sharp knife to sever the root and shoot from the seed. With the knife, gently cut open the seed case just enough to insert a freshly cut scion into the opening. To fit the scion snugly inside the seed cavity, trim its base to a wedge shape (see illustration). With the scion, bury the seed in a soil mixture of equal parts moist sand and peat moss so that the union of seed and scion is 1 inch below the surface.

A seed flat is an excellent container for starting a number of these grafts. Enclose the whole flat in a loose, clear plastic bag to maintain high humidity. You'll know the procedure has been successful when the tiny leaf buds on the cuttings (scions) begin to unfurl.

This system has a higher rate of success than ordinary cutting methods, because the scions obtain food and growth hormones from the seed.

Grafting   Producing flowering camellias from seed or cuttings is a slow process. One way to get flowering plants in a much shorter time is by grafting. Although it may take six years for a rooted cutting to flower, a graft will probably flower in two years. This propagation procedure requires a rootstock, which can be any species of camellia with a healthy root system and several inches of main stem. *C. sasanqua* and *C. japonica* are the most popular choices as rootstocks because their roots are relatively hardy. Check with your local nursery or camellia society about obtaining rootstock.

Grafting can be done indoors under glass (beginning in December) or outdoors in shaded nursery beds, pots, or in the garden (beginning in February or March), depending on the climate. The rootstock should be ¼ inch or larger in diameter. Cut the scion—the part that fits into the rootstock—from the mature wood of the previous season. When you slip the scion into the rootstock, it is essential to position the graft so that the cambium layer of the scion (the green band) matches the cambium layer of the rootstock. See the illustrations for grafting details. Keep the graft moist by placing a wide-mouthed glass jar over it (though a clear plastic bag over a suitable support is acceptable in sheltered locations). If the scion feels loosely fitted rather than firmly wedged, bind it tight with a piece of waxed cord, tape, or a rubber band. Label the graft with the name of the rootstock and the name of the scion, and protect it from direct sunlight by covering the jar with a paper bag until a good callus has formed to seal the union. Gradually expose the graft to more light and air by slowly tilting the jar. Carefully, transfer the graft to a shaded temporary nursery bed after the scion has produced a healthy set of leaves, and remove any suckers (side shoots sprouting from the rootstock). Do not transplant the new graft to a permanent location until the plant is at least a year old.

To keep newly struck grafts moist under indoor conditions, cover them with plastic bags supported by wire hoops. Cover with a paper bag to reduce heat accumulation inside the plastic. Remove the plastic bags gradually, by punching holes in the plastic. More grafts are probably lost because of sudden exposure to the air than for any other reason.

Air layering This is a propagation method for producing good-sized plants in one year. It may be done at any time of the year, but the best time is in the early spring, when the plants are beginning to grow. In air layering, the rooting medium is air instead of soil.

On a healthy limb, measure back 12 to 18 inches from the tip of the branch. At this point, completely remove a ring of bark. The strip of bark should be 1½ to 2 times the diameter of the branch to be air-layered. An easy way to do this is to make two parallel cuts with scissors or a sharp knife, then lift the strip off. Though the branch may be producing new growth, the wood where the bark is removed should be hardened off.

Eliminate all traces of the cambium layer (green tissue) by scraping with a knife. Dust the exposed surface with a rooting hormone powder recommended for hardwood cuttings. Cover the ringed area with a handful of pre-soaked sphagnum moss from which the excess water has been squeezed. Wrap this tightly with medium-weight plastic and secure with twist ties above and below the ball of moss. Cover this ball with a square of aluminum foil.

Air layers started in the early spring have usually formed roots by late summer or fall. Feeder roots will be visible through the plastic. When the roots are visible through the moss, use sharp clippers to cut the limb from the mother plant, at the lower edge of the moss. Then remove the plastic. Do not remove the moss; it protects the tender roots. For best results, plant the rooted limb in a container until it has a chance to produce more growth.

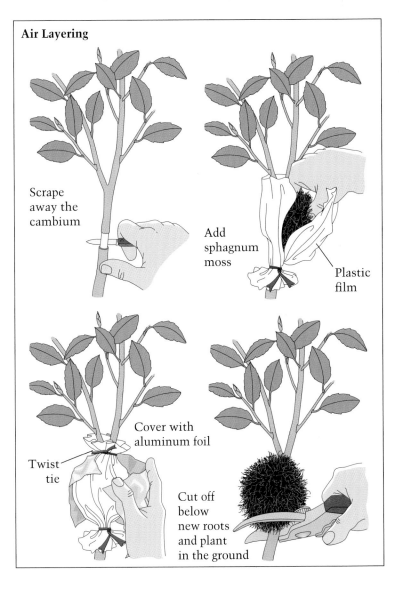

Air Layering

Scrape away the cambium

Add sphagnum moss

Plastic film

Twist tie

Cover with aluminum foil

Cut off below new roots and plant in the ground

Pests, Diseases, and Disorders

PESTS
Like all other plants, rhododendrons, azaleas, and camellias are subject to various plant pests, diseases, and cultural problems. Most pests, diseases, and cultural problems are easy to control. Here are the common symptoms, diagnoses, and treatments.

Black Vine Weevil and Strawberry Root Weevil
Affected plants   Rhododendrons and azaleas.

Symptoms   The leaf margins may be scalloped or notched, and the leaves may be yellowed, drooping, or curled. Look for areas at the base of the stem where the bark has been chewed. You may also find small (¼- to ½-inch-long) legless grubs (immature weevils) in the soil. If you inspect the plants at night, you may see black or grayish insects with snouts, ¼ to ⅜ inch long, on the leaves. These are the adult weevils.

Analysis   The larvae of these insects cause the most damage by feeding on plant roots. The adult weevils lay eggs close to the stem during summer, and the hatching larvae burrow into the soil. They injure the roots and often girdle the stem; they may cause wilting and death.

Treatment   Discard severely injured plants. Spray foliage and soil around adjacent healthy plants with an insecticide containing Orthene®. Repeat two or three times at intervals of three weeks. For complete control some plants may require treatment five or six times from May through September.

Lace Bugs
Affected plants   Rhododendrons and azaleas.

Symptoms   Leaves are speckled yellow and green, similar to mite-damaged leaves. Look for hard, black, shiny droplets on the undersides of damaged leaves, and small (⅛ inch) spiny wingless insects—the larvae—or brownish insects with large, clear lacy wings—the adults.

Analysis   Lace bugs suck sap from the undersides of leaves and leave black drops of excrement. These insects are more prevalent in sunny rather than shady conditions. The damage is unsightly and reduces plant vigor. Lace bugs are the most common insect problem on azaleas.

Treatment   Spray with an insecticide containing Orthene®. Be sure to cover the undersides of the leaves. Repeat 7 to 10 days later. A third application may even be necessary. Discourage lace bugs by hosing plants with strong jets of water and washing plants with insecticidal soaps. These procedures must be ongoing to keep populations down.

Rhododendron borer
Affected plants   Rhododendrons and azaleas.

Symptoms   Dime-sized spots dot the leaves. Leaves and shoots at the outer edge of the plant may wilt. Bark along the main stem and side branches flakes away easily, revealing tunnels and holes.

Analysis   Rhododendron borers are the larvae (caterpillars) of a moth common in the Atlantic Coast states. The yellowish white caterpillar is ½ inch long. It hatches from eggs laid on the bark, and burrows into the wood, working its way up the trunk and along the branches.

Treatment   Once inside the wood the borer is almost impossible to control, and the only remedy is to prune away all branches that show wilting. Take preventive measures early in the season by spraying or painting the trunk with an insecticide containing lindane to kill hatching larvae before they burrow. Repeat three more times at intervals of two weeks.

Scale
Affected plants   Camellias and occasionally rhododendrons and azaleas.

Symptoms   Bumps appear on the stems, branches, and leaves. They may be white, yellow, brown, gray, or reddish in color. The bumps can be scraped or picked off; the undersides are usually soft. Leaves turn yellow and branches die back. The plant may be dying.

Analysis   Many species of scale attack rhododendrons and azaleas. Scales are especially serious on camellias. Scales lay their eggs on leaves or bark in spring to midsummer. The young scales crawl to various parts of the plant, where they settle and begin feeding on plant sap. The legs usually atrophy and a hard crusty or waxy shell develops over the body. The tea scale is the most common and probably the most damaging insect pest of camellias.

Treatment Spray with an insecticide containing Orthene®. The following early spring, before new growth begins, spray the branches and trunk with a growing-season oil spray to control overwintering insects.

Spider mite

Affected plants Rhododendrons, azaleas, and camellias.

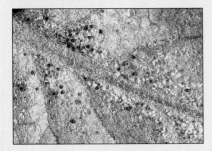

Symptoms Leaves become discolored and distorted, stippled yellow or bronze and dirty. There may be fine webs on the lower surfaces of leaves. For positive identification, hold a sheet of white paper beneath an affected leaf and tap the leaf sharply. Tiny green, red, or yellow specks the size of pepper grains will drop to the paper and crawl around.
Analysis Spider mites damage plants by sucking their sap. Mites are active throughout the growing season and are especially favored by hot, dry weather. Once infestations occur their effects are devastating, so administer controls as early as possible.
Treatment Spray with a pesticide containing Vendex®. Repeat the application if the plant becomes reinfested. Be sure to spray on the undersides of the leaves. You can also keep mite populations down by hosing plants with strong jets of water to dislodge webs and mites. To be effective, however, this must be an ongoing procedure.

Whiteflies

Affected plants Rhododendrons, azaleas, and camellias.

Symptoms Tiny, white, winged insects ($\frac{1}{12}$ inch long) appear on the undersides of leaves. When the plant is touched, the insects rise in a cloud and flutter around it. Leaves are mottled and yellowing. A sticky substance called honeydew coats the leaves, and a black sooty mold may grow on the honeydew.
Analysis The winged whitefly adult lays eggs on the undersides of leaves. The larvae are the size of a pinhead, flat, pale green, oval, and semitransparent. Both larvae and adults suck the sap of the plant, and excrete a sugary fluid called honeydew. Not a common problem except in greenhouses.
Treatment Spray with an insecticide containing Orthene® or diazinon. Repeat the spray two more times at intervals of 7 to 10 days. Thoroughly spray the upper and lower surfaces of the leaves.

DISEASES

Most diseases affecting rhododendrons and azaleas are caused by fungi. Since a particular disease can be highly localized, check with local nursery staff or your county extension office to determine which diseases are prevalent in your area. The diseases listed in this section are the most common.

Azalea petal blight

Affected plants Azaleas.

Symptoms Tiny circular spots form on the petals of azalea plants. The spots are pale or whitish on colored flowers, and rust-colored on white flowers. The spots enlarge, forming irregular patches, until the entire flower collapses. The petals feel slimy. Infected flowers dry up and cling to the plant. Small, dark, semicircular pellets—the resting stage of the fungus— may form on the petals.
Analysis Azalea petal blight is a serious fungal disease on azaleas in the humid coastal regions of the United States. Infected flowers decay rapidly. The dark fungal pellets produce spores in early spring that infect early-flowering plants. The fungus is especially destructive on azaleas in wet weather.
Treatment Spray the flowers with a fungicide containing triadimefon, chlorothalonil, or triforine. Test the fungicide on a few flowers before spraying the entire plant; some varieties may discolor. Repeat the spray every three to four days until flowering ends. Clean up and destroy litter around the base of the plants and pick off diseased flowers, if feasible. To prevent infection next year, begin spraying when the first color begins to show. Before flowering begins, spray the ground under the shrub with a fungicide containing PCNB.

Pests, Diseases, and Disorders (continued)

Camellia flower blight
Affected plants   Camellias.

Symptoms   Tan or brown spots or blotches spread across the flower, and the whole flower may turn brown and drop from the plant. The affected portions of the flower develop darkened veins in a netted pattern.

Analysis   This disease is caused by a fungus. Spores are carried to new flowers in late winter to early spring. If moisture is present, the fungus infects the flowers, which may turn completely brown within 48 hours.

Treatment   Pick off and destroy infected blossoms, and rake up and destroy old leaves, flowers, and plant debris. Spray the soil with a fungicide containing PCNB in December and repeat every three to four weeks throughout the blooming season. If camellia flower blight is especially severe in your area, protect the flowers with a spray containing benomyl as soon as they begin to show color. Repeat every three days to protect new flowers.

Dieback
Affected plants   Rhododendrons and azaleas.

Symptoms   Leaves and branch tips are wilted and dying. Leaves may turn reddish brown and remain attached to the plant, or the leaves may be rolled with spots that appear water-soaked. Often,

there are sunken, dead areas (cankers) at the base of the wilted branch.

Analysis   Dieback is a plant disease caused by several different fungi. The fungi enter the plant through wounds, dead and dying twigs, and leaves. They cause cankers to form that block off the flow of water and nutrients to the stems and branches above. Sometimes cankers do not form, but the fungi produce toxins that plug plant tissues.

Treatment   Once the branches are wilted and dying, there are no chemical cures. Prune out and destroy all affected branches. If the infection started with spotted leaves, protect the plant next year by spraying with chlorothalonil or a basic copper fungicide after blooming. Repeat the spray two more times at intervals of 14 days.

Powdery mildew
Affected plants   Deciduous azaleas.

Symptoms   The leaves, stems, and flowers are covered with patches of a grayish white, powdery material. New growth that is infected may become stunted and distorted. Leaves may discolor and die.

Analysis   Powdery mildew is caused by a fungus. The powdery layer consists of fungal strands and spores. The fungus saps plant nutrients, causing leaf discoloration and distortion.

Treatment   Spray with a fungicide containing dinocap. Rake up and destroy plant debris.

Root rot
Affected plants   Rhododendrons, azaleas, and camellias.

Symptoms   Young leaves turn yellow and wilt. Dead leaves remain attached to the plant and are rolled along the midrib. Tissue under the bark close to ground level shows a dark discoloration when the bark is cut or peeled back. There is a distinct line between diseased dark wood and healthy white wood. The plant may die.

Analysis   Root rot is caused by soil fungi that infect and destroy roots. Sometimes the fungi work their way up the stem. If they girdle the stem, the plant wilts and dies. Wet conditions favor the spread of the disease, which is most common in low-lying or poorly drained soils.

Treatment   Apply a fungicide containing metalaxyl to the soil; follow label instructions. Mildly affected plants may be saved by improving soil drainage. Preventive measures include planting in locations with well-drained soil and good air circulation. Plants grown in raised beds are less susceptible to the disease. Where root rot is a problem, plant species or varieties that are resistant to root rot, such as *C. sasanqua*.

DISORDERS

In addition to pests and diseases, there are several physiological disorders that can create symptoms on azaleas, camellias, and rhododendrons. These symptoms resemble those caused by pests and diseases. The major physiological disorders that the typical gardener is likely to encounter are described in this section.

Chlorosis

Affected plants Rhododendrons, azaleas, and camellias.

Symptoms Some of the leaves are pale green to yellow. The newest leaves may be completely yellow, with only the veins and the tissue right next to the veins remaining green.

Analysis Chlorosis is a common problem in acid-loving plants. It is caused by a deficiency of iron in plant tissues. The soil is seldom deficient in iron. However, iron is often found in an insoluble form that is not available to the plant, especially in soil with a pH of 7 or higher. Plants located near cement paths or walls, especially in naturally alkaline areas, are likely to develop chlorosis.

Treatment Increase the acidity of the soil by adding ferrous sulfate, aluminum sulfate, ammonium sulfate, or sulfur (check the soil pH after each application—add more if needed). Amend the soil with peat moss or leaf mold, and use a fertilizer formulated for acid-loving plants. If the problem is severe, spray the foliage with chelated iron.

Salt burn

Affected plants Rhododendrons, azaleas, and camellias.

Symptoms Leaf edges are brown and dead. Browning usually occurs on older leaves first. This distinguishes the problem from windburn, which develops on young, exposed leaves first.

Analysis Salt burn occurs when excess soil salts are taken up by the plant and accumulate in the leaves. This problem is most common in areas of low rainfall and where too much fertilizer has been applied. Salt burn can also occur in plants growing in poorly drained soils or containers.

Treatment The damage will not disappear from the affected leaves, but injury can be avoided in the future. In areas of low rainfall, leach accumulated salts from the soil with an occasional heavy irrigation (about once a month). Improve soil drainage to allow salts to leach away more easily. Flush excess salts from container soils by watering the plant heavily several times in a row. Do not overfertilize, and water thoroughly after fertilizer applications, to prevent salt buildup.

Windburn and winter injury

Affected plants Rhododendrons, azaleas, and camellias.

Symptoms Young and exposed leaves are brown and dry, especially around the leaf edges and near the tips. One side of the plant may look healthy while the other side looks sick. The shrub is planted in a windy location or is growing in a cold climate where cold, dry, windy days are common.

Analysis Windburn and winter injury are common on plants growing in windswept locations. When winter temperatures drop below freezing, strong winds cause leaves to lose moisture more rapidly than the root system can replace it. The damage may not appear for several weeks. Leaf burn also occurs on exceptionally windy, dry summer days.

Treatment If the damage is localized, prune away affected limbs. To prevent further damage, plant shrubs in locations protected from wind or provide temporary winter windbreaks of burlap over a wooden frame. Plants should be well watered during hot, windy weather. Water in late fall or winter, if necessary, to ensure adequate soil moisture.

Harvesting the reward for keeping plants healthy—vibrant blooms.

Encyclopedia of Rhododendrons, Azaleas, and Camellias

Here you will find hundreds of spectacular azaleas, camellias, and rhododendrons.

The first part of this book has introduced you to rhododendrons, azaleas, and camellias—their special beauty, their general uses in the garden, and their cultural needs and maintenance requirements. The following encyclopedia describes hundreds of rhododendrons, azaleas, and camellias. This is not an exhaustive list—there are several thousands of hybrids. But many of the most widely available and choicest plants are listed here. As long as you live in an area where rhododendrons, azaleas, or camellias will grow, you're sure to find a great number of plants that will suit your particular climate and landscaping needs perfectly. Because rhododendrons, azaleas, and camellias are long-lived and often develop into large, woody shrubs, they are used as permanent plantings. So, as you make your selections, carefully consider the characteristics of the plants and how they will grow in your garden, especially when they reach full size. There are many factors to consider when selecting plants for your garden.

•Select plants that are adapted to your climate and the conditions within your garden. Prepare your soil properly, and improve the drainage if necessary (see pages 26 and 27).

•Evaluate the landscape qualities of the plants you select. Plant habit is important. The effect of a loose, open, upright growth habit is entirely different from that of a dense, spreading growth habit. Pay attention to the plant's mature size—and how quickly it will grow to that size. Remember that the sizes given in the encyclopedia are approximate. Plants in mild climates, such as that of the Pacific Northwest, enjoy a longer growing season, and tend to grow a little bit larger than those in colder areas. Consider how the color of the flowers will blend with other flower and foliage colors in your garden. Your plant will not

A casual mix of rhododendrons brightens the edge of a garden.

have flowers much of the year, so think about the quality of the foliage. Take into account the color, texture, and shape of the leaves; the appearance of new growth; and, in the case of rhododendrons and azaleas, the downiness or indumentum (plant hairs) on the undersides of the leaves.

•Purchase named plants from a reliable local garden center or mail-order nursery. Often, plants sold by color name—red, pink, or some other color—may be seedlings that are inferior to selected named cultivars or varieties.

ENCYCLOPEDIA ORGANIZATION

The encyclopedia is divided into three sections: rhododendrons, azaleas, and camellias. Each of these sections is further divided into subsections. Use the mini-index, which follows, to quickly locate the page where each subsection starts. Most of the subsections contain lists of hybrids. In these lists, the entries are listed alphabetically by their cultivar names, such as 'Scintillation' or 'Pink Perfection'; the genus and species names do not appear. These are the names you would ask for when visiting a local nursery or ordering from a mail-order company. If you know the name of a particular species or hybrid, use the index to find the plant.

Plant Description

Each entry describes the plant's most noteworthy characteristics. In most cases, you'll find descriptions of the flower color and size, and details about leaf size and shape, growth habit, mature plant size, and cold hardiness. Sometimes hybridizers' names or groups of hybrids are included in the description of a particular plant.

A wild azalea, Rhododendron kiusianum, *grows on a Japanese hillside.*

Adaptation Maps

Each plant or group of plants is accompanied by a map of the United States. The map is divided into three adaptation areas.

Adaptation area 1 (blue on the map)

Well adapted. The plant can be grown outdoors with a minimum of care. Supplemental watering and feeding may be required. Climate protection is not required for survival of the plant, but it may be used to extend the growing season.

Adaptation area 2 (red on the map)

Marginally adapted. The plant can be grown outdoors with more care than is given to well-adapted plants. Climate protection may be required for survival.

Adaptation area 3 (uncolored part of the map)

Not adapted. Does not survive or produce flowers outdoors. May be grown as a greenhouse plant or as a container plant that is wintered indoors.

America

Autumn Gold

RHODODENDRONS

Rhododendrons are best known for their dramatic, colorful flowers, but they are also very valuable as landscape plants. From compact, sun-loving shrubs perfect for the rock garden to small, understory trees, rhododendrons are available in a tremendous variety of sizes and shapes.

Rhododendrons are divided into three categories: rhododendron hybrids, rhododendron species, and Vireya rhododendrons. Plant heights are provided for all of the rhododendron entries. They are as follows.
Dwarf: under 2 feet
Low: 2 to 4 feet
Medium: 4 to 6 feet
Tall: over 6 feet

Rhododendron Hybrids

Hybrid rhododendrons can be divided into two groups, lepidote (those with scaly leaves) and elepidote (those with nonscaly leaves). The following list of hybrids includes some of the more popular varieties available today.

Elepidote

The elepidote rhododendron hybrids are large-leaved—4 to 8 inches or more in length. The leaves are generally smooth, but many have a thick fuzz called indumentum on the undersides of the leaves.

A. Bedford
(syn. 'Anne Bedford' and 'Arthur Bedford')

This large, beautiful plant is especially suitable as a background plant. The flowers are a pale to light purple, offset by a distinct dark purplish red blotch. The flowers are funnel-shaped, 3 inches wide, with slightly ruffled petals. Up to 16 flowers may appear on the dome-shaped, compact trusses. The plants are vigorous with large dark glossy leaves about 6 inches long. Tall, hardy to –5° F.

Album Elegans

This old cold-hardy Iron Clad hybrid has newly opening flowers of white tinged with light purple, quickly fading to pure white as they continue to open. An attractive, greenish yellow blotch spots the flower throats. The flowers are about 2½ inches wide, and are borne in tight, rounded trusses. The plant is tall and vigorous, with a fairly open growth habit. 'Album Grandiflorum' is similar but has a slightly larger white flower with an olive-brown blotch. Hardy to –20° F.

America

This Iron Clad hybrid has small dark red flowers 1½ inches wide and borne in tight rounded trusses. The leaves are heavily veined, green, and 4 inches long. This low to medium shrub has an open growth habit and develops its best form in full sun. Hardy to –20° F.

Anah Kruschke

This attractive compact hardy plant tolerates sun and heat well. The light reddish purple flowers are 3 inches wide, and are borne in cone-shaped trusses. The dark green leaves are 5 inches long, and the foliage is dense. Medium, hardy to 10° F.

Anna Rose Whitney

The deep pink funnel-shaped flowers of this popular Van Veen hybrid are 3 to 4 inches wide. The large, slightly open trusses may carry 12 or more flowers. It is a large, heat-tolerant and vigorous plant with attractive dense green foliage and an upright growth habit. The leaves are 6 to 8 inches long. This lovely plant needs plenty of room and looks best in a large garden. Tall, hardy to –5° F.

Autumn Gold

This Van Veen hybrid has distinct late-blooming flowers of strong salmon pink with an orange throat, in trusses of 10 flowers. This large shrub has dense foliage and light green leaves 5 inches long. It performs best in partial shade. Medium, hardy to –5° F.

Blue Peter

Boule de Neige

Belle Heller

The beautiful pure white flowers of this Shammarello hybrid are 3 to 4 inches wide and have a vivid yellow blotch. The trusses are large and globular. A large, vigorous, sun-tolerant plant with good foliage, 'Belle Heller' often flowers in the fall in warm climates. Medium, hardy to –10° F.

Besse Howells

This compact, medium-cold–hardy shrub, with lustrous green foliage, was also introduced by Shammarello. The attractive, frilled, red flowers, 2½ inches wide with dark red blotches, are borne in a globular truss. Occasionally flowers in the fall in warm climates. Low, hardy to –20° F.

Betty Wormald

This old hybrid is a vigorous plant with an upright, spreading growth habit. The large, slightly frilled, light pink flowers have pale centers and a dark blotch on the upper petal. The blooms are 3 to 4 inches across, and are almost flat when fully open. Trusses are large, showy, and dome-shaped. Medium to tall, hardy to –5° F.

Blue Peter

This popular Waterer hybrid has frilled flowers of a very light purple with a dark purple blotch. The plant is a vigorous grower with glossy, green, dense foliage. A reliable, cold-hardy, and heat-resistant plant, 'Blue Peter' is a favorite in the eastern United States. Medium, hardy to –20° F.

Bob Bovee

This medium, compact Bovee hybrid has pinkish flower buds that open to pale yellow blossoms, 3 inches wide, with spotted red to greenish

throats. Each truss bears 10 to 12 flowers. The leaves are 4 to 5 inches long. Plants are hardy to –10° F.

Boule de Neige

An old Iron Clad, this hybrid is popular in the Northeast for its cold hardiness and rounded growth habit. The snowy white flowers are borne in tight trusses. The plant is heat tolerant and can be used in full sun. 'Boule de Neige' is especially susceptible to lace bug. Where this insect is a problem, grow the plant in partial shade. Low to medium, hardy to –25° F.

Bow Bells

This beautiful plant was introduced by L. de Rothschild. The contrast of the deep pink buds with the fully open lighter pink, bell-shaped flowers creates a striking two-toned effect against the dark green foliage. The new growth is reddish orange, adding to the colorful springtime display. The compact, rounded plant is best

used in partial shade. With time, it may eventually reach 6 feet. Low, hardy to –5° F.

Caroline

This hardy Gable hybrid grows well in both hot and cold climates. It bears pale purplish-pink, lightly scented flowers on large trusses. The dark green leaves are 6 inches long with wavy margins. Medium, hardy to –20° F.

Catagla

This very cold-hardy Gable Nearing hybrid has large trusses of flowers that are light pink in bud, opening to clear white. A popular plant for hybridizing in the Northeast. Medium to tall, hardy to –25° F.

Crest

Daphnoides

Catawbiense Album

A vigorous, cold-hardy Iron Clad, this hybrid has flowers that are tinted pale purple in bud and open to pure white with a spotted greenish blotch. The plant is covered with dark green, slightly convex large leaves 6 inches long. Medium to tall, hardy to −25° F.

Cheer

This Shammarello hybrid blooms early, bearing light to medium pink flowers. The blooms are 2½ inches wide with a conspicuous scarlet blotch, and are borne in conical trusses. The glossy leaves are 4 to 5 inches long, and the growth habit is dense, compact, and mounding. Plants are heat tolerant and occasionally flower in fall in warmer climates. Low, hardy to −10° F.

Christmas Cheer

A hardy, medium-sized plant. The pink buds fade to very light pink flowers that bloom in March. Hardy to −10° F.

Cotton Candy

This spectacular hybrid was developed for the Northwest. The pastel pink flowers fade to an even lighter pink center, and the flower buds are dark pink; the contrast of the lighter open flowers against the darker buds results in an attractive two-toned effect. The blooms are large, ranging from 4 to 5 inches wide, and are carried on large, tall, upright trusses. A top-rated plant of vigorous growth with large, dark green, glossy leaves 6 inches long. Medium, hardy to 5° F.

County of York
(syn. 'Catalode')

This is a good cold-hardy and heat-tolerant Gable hybrid. The white flowers are 4 inches wide, have a conspicuous olive throat, and are carried in a large upright truss. A vigorous large plant with glossy, dark green leaves 8 to 11 inches long. Tall, hardy to −15° F.

Crest

One of the first good yellow rhododendrons, this hybrid was introduced by L. de Rothschild. The large, light yellow flowers are borne in a large truss. Young plants are slow to set flower buds but, once established, set buds freely. A vigorous plant with a habit of growth so open that many of the branches are exposed, 'Crest' replaces all of its leaves yearly. Despite some of its faults, it is still the standard by which newer yellow hybrids are evaluated. Tall, hardy to −5° F.

Cynthia

This old favorite has large, rounded trusses consisting of more than two hundred deep pink flowers. The vigorous upright plant tolerates heat and sun. In shade, its growth habit is fairly open; in sun, it's more compact. Tall, hardy to −10° F.

Daphnoides

An old variety, this plant is noted for its dense, glossy, rolled foliage, with leaves 4 inches long. The small, light purple flowers make a tight rounded truss. This slow-growing, heat-resistant plant develops a compact habit of growth. Low to medium, hardy to −10° F.

Cynthia

Elizabeth

Dexter's Appleblossom

This vigorous Dexter hybrid produces large, six-lobed, fragrant flowers held in flat trusses. The white blooms are edged with pink, spotted with a yellowish green blotch, and 3 inches wide. The foliage is dark green. Tall, hardy to –5° F.

Dexter's Cream

The fragrant flowers of this Dexter hybrid are pale yellowish white shaded with pink. These six-lobed blooms are 3½ inches wide, held in open trusses. Leaves are small, only 3½ inches long. Low, hardy to 0° F.

Dexter's Orange

The seven-lobed flowers are pink with a brownish orange blotch. The flowers are 3 inches wide, and are held in an open truss of eight florets. The medium-sized leaves are 4½ inches long. Low, hardy to 0° F.

Dexter's Spice

The fragrant blooms are white with a pale yellow-green spotted blotch. Each flower has seven lobes, and is 5 inches wide. The leaves may reach 7 inches in length. Medium, hardy to 0° F.

Dexter's Springtime

This hybrid bears yellowish white flowers edged in deep pink, with reddish brown dots in the blotch. The blooms are fragrant, six-lobed, 3½ inches wide, and borne in flat trusses. Dwarf to low, hardy to 0° F.

Elizabeth

One of the finest compact dwarf rhododendrons, this hybrid is especially well suited to the West. The large, bright red flowers are trumpet-shaped and often cover the entire plant. Each truss bears six to nine flowers. The plant blooms early and may be subject to some late frost damage. The

small, dark green leaves range from 2½ to 3½ inches in length. Dwarf to low, hardy to 0° F.

English Roseum

This old Iron Clad is still popular in the East but seldom used in the West. Large trusses carry rosy lavender flowers 1½ inches wide. 'English Roseum' is a good plant for beginners. It is vigorous with smooth, glossy leaves, and it tolerates heat and extreme humidity. Tall, hardy to –25° F.

Evening Glow

A compact, medium-sized plant with light green leaves. The late-blooming flowers are yellow on a very lax truss. Hardy to –5° F.

Faggetter's Favourite

Deep pink buds open to a yellowish white tinged with pink; the throat is speckled with brown. The slightly fragrant flowers are 3½ inches wide, and are borne in large trusses. The plant is vigorous, yet it maintains a compact habit. For best performance, provide some shade. Tall, hardy to 0° F.

Gi Gi

This popular Dexter hybrid has flowers that are deep pink with dark red spots, and are 3¼ inches wide. Each truss bears 18 flowers. The glossy leaves are 4½ inches long. Medium, hardy to –5° F.

Goldfort

This is a cold-hardy yellow hybrid. Pink buds open to pale yellow flowers, 3 inches wide. The throat is a darker yellow with faint dots of green. Foliage is yellowish green. Medium, hardy to –10° F.

Gi Gi

Janet Blair

Goldsworth Yellow

One of the oldest yellow hybrids, this plant was introduced in England in 1925. The floral buds are light orange, opening to pale light yellow with reddish dots in the throat. It's an old standard for yellows but difficult to propagate and gradually being replaced. Medium, hardy to –15° F.

Gomer Waterer

An old Iron Clad, this hybrid is still popular in the East. The buds are pale pink, opening to a clear white with a faint green blotch. The late-blooming flowers are 3 inches wide, and are carried in large trusses. This plant is very tolerant of sun and heat, and it has attractive foliage. Medium to large, hardy to –15° F.

Halfdan Lem

This award-winning hybrid by Lem has bright red flowers, 3½ inches wide, marked with a darker blotch and borne in large, tight trusses. The leaves are large, broad, deep green, and 8 inches long. The hybrid is excellent in the Northwest, but mostly untried in the East. Medium to large, hardy to –5° F.

Hello Dolly

Another beautiful hybrid, this is a favorite in the Northwest. The flowers are two-toned and often called yellow, but they are actually a yellowish pink blending to yellow in the throat with a few light green dots, 2¾ inches wide. The leaves are medium green with light beige indumentum on the undersides, and the growth habit is rounded. Low, hardy to –10° F.

Holden

This hardy, compact Shammarello hybrid is popular in the Midwest and Northeast. The deep pink flowers marked with red blotches are 2½ inches wide and borne in cone-shaped trusses. Leaves are a lustrous dark green and 4 inches long. 'Holden' is heat tolerant, but it flowers in fall in the Southeast. Medium, hardy to –15° F.

Hotei

The brilliant yellow flowers are broadly cup-shaped, 2½ inches wide, and carried in a rounded truss. The growth habit is compact. Requires good drainage. Medium, hardy to –5° F.

Janet Blair

The petals of this David Leach introduction (often incorrectly called 'John Wister') are pink and distinctly frilled, and the blooms are 3½

inches wide. A wide-growing plant with attractive foliage, 'Janet Blair' is vigorous and heat tolerant. Tall, hardy to –15° F.

Jean Marie de Montague

This beautiful old favorite from Holland is often listed as 'Jean Marie' and was originally registered as 'The Honorable Jean Marie de Montague'. The vivid scarlet flowers are in large trusses. The plant bears bright, dark green foliage and tolerates sun and heat. Medium, hardy to about –10° F.

King of Shrubs

The large, apricot yellow flowers of this popular plant are edged with a wide band of pink, and the 3-inch blooms are borne in open trusses. The narrow pointed leaves are 2 inches wide and from 5 to 6 inches long. Medium, hardy to 0° F.

Lem's Cameo

Loderi King George

Lee's Dark Purple

An old reliable hybrid particularly suited to the Southwest. The flowers are dark purple and bloom in the fall in the Deep South. The plant is vigorous and heat resistant, with dark green, wavy leaves. Tall, hardy to –15° F.

Lem's Cameo

This spectacular plant is one of the few to receive the Superior Plant Award. The flowers are light yellow suffused with pink and 3 to 4 inches wide. Each large domed truss may carry up to 20 flowers. The new foliage has a reddish tint that changes to a glossy green. Particularly suited to the Northwest, it may be hard to find because it is difficult to propagate. Medium, hardy to 5° F.

Lem's Monarch

This breathtakingly beautiful hybrid is a recipient of the Award of Excellence and is a must for gardens in the Northwest. The large (3- to 4-inch) flowers are light pink edged with deep pink, and are borne in large spectacular trusses. The plant is vigorous, and the large leaves are dark green. 'Pink Walloper' and 'Lem's Monarch' are considered the same plant. Tall, reported hardy to –5° F, but tender in the East.

Loderi King George

This is an outstanding hybrid. The fragrant flowers are pale pink in bud, opening to white, and 3 to 5 inches wide. It is a very large shrub or small tree with excellent foliage, and performs best with some shelter from sun and wind. Best seen in England and in protected areas of the Northwest. There are ten or more Loderi cultivars. ('Loderi Pink Diamond', with pale pink flowers, is similar to 'Loderi King George'.) Tall, hardy to 5° F.

Mars

This old reliable hybrid has deep red flowers with contrasting white stamens. It is a compact plant with dark green, waxy, ribbed leaves. 'Mars' grows in partial shade protected from hot sun. Medium, hardy to –10° F.

Mission Bells

The pale pink flowers are bell-shaped, 2½ inches wide, slightly fragrant, and borne in an open truss. The plant is compact, with glossy foliage and small leaves. It is more common in the West because it is sun tolerant. Low, hardy to –5° F.

Mrs. Furnival

This is a spectacular plant in flower. The light pink flowers have a distinct splashy red blotch and are borne in large dome-shaped trusses. It is vigorous with attractive foliage and large leaves. It is a beautiful plant in western gardens and can be grown with protection in the East. Medium, hardy to –10° F.

Nova Zembla

This old Iron Clad hybrid has red flowers, 1½ inches wide, borne in a tight truss. This vigorous, tough plant is noted for its cold hardiness and heat tolerance. Medium, hardy to –25° F.

Noyo Brave

This hybrid has pink flowers, 2½ inches wide, marked with a small red blotch. The rounded trusses may bear up to 22 flowers. Low, hardy to 5° F.

Noyo Chief

President Roosevelt

Noyo Chief
Recipient of the Award of Excellence, this hybrid bears vivid red, ruffled flowers, 2½ inches wide, on tight, compact trusses. It is a compact plant with excellent foliage: glossy, dark green, ribbed leaves with a beautiful tan indumentum. This hybrid is best in the Northwest. Also known as 'Zeylanicum'. Medium, hardy to 10° F.

Odee Wright
This is a beautiful hybrid from the West Coast. The large, vivid yellow flowers, 4½ inches wide with a reddish throat, are borne in a large truss. The buds are a contrasting light reddish orange. A compact grower with wavy, dark green leaves, this hybrid has seldom been evaluated in the East. Medium, hardy to –5° F.

Old Copper
This Van Veen hybrid bears large copper-colored flowers in a loose truss. The medium-sized plant has long dark green leaves. Medium, hardy to –5° F.

Pink Pearl
This old but well-known English hybrid is excellent in the Northwest. Large, soft pink flowers are borne in good-sized trusses. It is a vigorous plant with an open habit of growth and light green foliage. Tall, reported hardy to –5° F in the Northwest, but best used in protected sites.

Pink Twins
This cold-hardy Gable hybrid has attractive, shrimp pink, hose-in-hose flowers 2 inches wide. The blooms are carried in tight dome-shaped trusses. The dark green leaves have a distinct contrasting yellow petiole. Medium, hardy to –15° F.

Pink Walloper
This Lem hybrid thrives in the Northwest. Red buds open to large, deep pink flowers, gradually fading to a lighter shade. The blooms are carried in gigantic trusses, which are well balanced by large-leafed, handsome foliage. There are several color forms, including red, pink, and rose. Tall, hardy to –5° F.

Point Defiance
This spectacular hybrid has large, white flowers, 4½ inches wide, with a beautiful deep pink margin that becomes lighter toward the center. The plant is best used in northwestern gardens. Medium to tall, hardy to –5° F.

President Roosevelt
This striking plant shows variegation in both flowers and foliage. The frilly, cherry red flowers have a white center, and the dark green leaves are blotched with yellow and occasionally have yellow margins. This shrub works well as an accent plant because of its interesting foliage. It is best used in full sun. Medium, hardy to 0° F.

Purple Splendour
This popular old hybrid has strikingly dark flowers of deep purple marked with a black blotch. The growth habit is compact, and the leaves are dark green. Give this plant good drainage. Medium to large, hardy to –5° F.

Roseum Elegans

Scintillation

Roseum Elegans

A good, cold-hardy Iron Clad, the plant has deep purplish pink flowers, 1½ inches wide, borne in large trusses. It is a vigorous shrub with medium green foliage. One of the easiest to grow, it is a good plant for beginners in the East and West. 'Roseum Superbum' is very similar. Tall, hardy to –25° F.

Sappho

This old, popular variety is noted for its flower blotches. The white flowers are marked with a distinctive deep purple blotch. 'Sappho' is vigorous with medium, narrow, olive green leaves. Tall, hardy to –10° F.

Scarlet Wonder

The flowers of this aptly named hybrid are vivid scarlet and are held in loose, open trusses. The foliage is glossy, textured, and dense. The growth habit is compact, and the plant tolerates heat and sun well. Low, hardy to –15° F.

Scintillation

One of the best known of the Dexter hybrids, 'Scintillation' received the Award of Excellence. The slightly fragrant flowers are pale to light pink, with a distinct blotch of brownish bronze dots. Blooms are 2½ inches wide, and are borne in large trusses of 12 to 15 flowers. This vigorous and sturdy plant is heat tolerant, and has dark, waxy, shiny foliage with leaves up to 6 inches long. Medium to tall, hardy to –5° F.

Sham's Candy

This Shammarello introduction has dark pink flowers marked with a yellow-green blotch, 2¼ inches wide, and carried in a conical truss. The vigorous plant has yellowish green foliage with leaves 4½ inches long. Medium, hardy to –20° F.

Sham's Juliet

Another cold-hardy Shammarello introduction, this hybrid has light pink flowers edged with a darker shade of pink and marked with brownish dots in the throat. The 2½-inch-wide flowers are borne in a rounded truss. Foliage is dark green, and the leaves are 3¼ to 4 inches long. Low to medium, hardy to –20° F.

Trude Webster

This super plant, a Greer hybrid, received a Superior Plant Award. The huge flowers, 5 inches wide, are clear pink with faint reddish specks in the blotch. Dark green leaves grow to 7 inches in length and 3 inches in width. Although heat tolerant, it grows best in partial shade. Medium to large, hardy to –10° F.

Virginia Richards

This is a beautiful Whitney hybrid. As the pink buds open, they fade to an even lighter pink, then change to a pale yellowish pink with a faint orange tint. The base of the throat is red with a blotch of reddish dots. The blooms are large, about 4½ inches wide. 'Virginia Richards' is a vigorous, compact grower with dark green, glossy leaves 4½ inches long. A word of caution: Several forms sold under the same name do not produce the same interesting bloom. Low to medium, hardy to –5° F.

Vulcan

This very popular hybrid has fiery red flowers, 2½ inches wide, in a heavy domelike truss. The compact shrub features dark, glossy foliage and is heat tolerant. Several forms of 'Vulcan' are available, including 'Vulcan Flame'. Medium, hardy to –10° F.

Trude Webster

Vulcan

Wheatly

This Dexter hybrid is popular in the East. The fragrant, fluorescent pink flowers are outlined by a margin of deep pink and accented by a splash of yellow-green in the throat. Blooms are carried in large trusses containing as many as 16 blossoms. The sturdy, compact plant has large, dark green leaves up to 7 inches long. Medium to large, hardy to –10° F.

Wissahickon

Especially popular in the East, this Dexter hybrid features large trusses of deep pink blossoms that hold up well in the sun. The attractive foliage is dark green, with an open habit. Medium to tall, hardy to –15° F.

Yaku Prince

This dwarf cultivar, introduced by Shammarello, inherits its name from one of its parents, *R. yakushimanum.* The purple flowers, 2¼ inches wide, sport a pale pink blotch flecked with reddish orange. Spherical trusses hold from 14 to 16 blooms. Hardy to –10° F.

Lepidote hybrids

Lepidote rhododendrons have small leaves, usually less than 4 inches long. The leaves are scaly, particularly on the underside. The scales appear as small dots to the naked eye. Although only a few lepidote hybrids existed a century ago, they are becoming more numerous, and are valuable garden plants. Many are hardier than the elepidote hybrids and offer an interesting change of foliage color from summer to winter. Early leaders in lepidote hybrids in the United States include Ed Mezitt, Guy Nearing, and Joseph Gable.

Ann Carey

A hybrid most commonly seen in the Northwest, this variety has a very interesting flower that opens chartreuse then changes to a yellowish pink. The small flowers are 1 inch wide and have petal-like stamens; the trusses develop from the tips and along the sides of the stems; the leaves are small, about 3 inches long. Low to medium, hardy to 5° F.

Blue Diamond

This old favorite is an effective accent plant. The small flowers, 1½ inches wide, are light violet with a bluish tint. It is a dense, compact plant with small leaves 1½ inches long, and it grows best in the Northwest and in full sun. 'Blue Ridge', a new cultivar similar to 'Blue Diamond', is more cold-hardy. Low, hardy to 0° F.

Conewago

This Gable hybrid has small, purplish pink flowers. The growth habit is open and upright, and the leaves are small. Similar sister seedlings are 'Conemaugh' and 'Conestoga'. Low, hardy to –25° F.

Cornell Pink

Often called an azalea, this is a true rhododendron. The flowers are a true pink. Blooms open to form flattened trumpets, 1½ to 2 inches wide. This early-flowering shrub is deciduous with small leaves. It is often used with forsythia to create an interesting early display of color. Medium to tall, hardy to –25° F.

Dora Amaties

Windbeam

Dora Amaties

This recipient of the Award of Excellence has white flowers, 2 inches wide, lightly spotted with green in the blotch, and borne in small clusters of five. The small, bushy shrub has dark green leaves up to 2½ inches long that develop a bronze color in the winter. The plant works well in a mass planting and is frequently planted in front of larger shrubs. Low, hardy to –15° F.

Mary Fleming

This delightfully colored Nearing hybrid is also a recipient of the Award of Excellence. The early-blooming flowers are a pale orange-yellow streaked with pink. The blooms are 1¼ inches wide and borne in small trusses, and are susceptible to discoloration by a late frost. The leaves, 1½ inches long, turn reddish brown in winter. Low, hardy to –15° F.

Pioneer

This hardy Gable hybrid has light to purplish pink flowers, 1½ inches wide, borne in profusion. The growth habit is upright, and the small leaves are semievergreen to deciduous in cold climates. 'Pioneer' flowers very early, usually after 'Cornell Pink'. Low to medium, hardy to –20° F.

P.J.M.

The vivid purple-pink flowers of this popular cold-hardy Mezitt hybrid are 1½ inches wide. Blooms appear early in small clusters. Dark green leaves up to 3½ inches long turn a reddish brown in the winter. Best in full sun, the plant is heat tolerant but often blooms in the fall in milder climates. Two similar new varieties that do not bloom in the fall are 'Olga' (medium pink) and 'Victor' (light purplish pink). Medium, hardy to –30° F.

Ramapo

A hardy dwarf Nearing hybrid, 'Ramapo' has small, light purple flowers that appear early and may cover the entire plant. The small oval leaves are bluish green, 1 inch long, and new growth is dusky blue. It is excellent in a rock garden or as a border or edging plant. 'Ramapo' rarely grows taller than 2 feet. It remains especially compact when grown in sun, which it tolerates in cooler climates. Unfortunately, the plant is not reliably heat tolerant. Dwarf, hardy to –25° F.

Shamrock

This exciting and unusual dwarf hybrid has small, chartreuse flowers 1½ inches wide, and it blooms right around St. Patrick's Day. It is a very compact plant that grows wider than high, and it has small, light green leaves 1¾ inches long. 'Shamrock' looks striking planted in combination with other early dwarf early purple hybrids. Dwarf, hardy to –5° F.

Windbeam

This popular Nearing hybrid has flowers that are apricot yellow in bud, change to pale pink, and then become almost white when fully open. Blooms are small, about 1 inch wide, and appear early in the season. The growth habit is compact, and the small, dark leaves, 2½ inches long, change to a reddish brown in winter. 'Windbeam' tolerates heat well. Low, hardy to –25° F.

Rhododendron carolinianum

Rhododendron keiskei

Rhododendron fortunei

Rhododendron Species

In addition to the large number of rhododendron hybrids, there are several species out of the more than eight hundred rhododendron species known worldwide that are suitable for the home gardener. These rhododendron species range from very small dwarf varieties to trees over 80 feet high, with foliage and flowers of great diversity. Several of these species are native to North America. The interest in rhododendron species is increasing as the interest in native plants increases. The following are just a few of the many rhododendron species available from either local nurseries or specialty mail-order sources (see page 92).

R. augustinii

The flowers of this bushy shrub from China are often described as blue, but they actually vary from light to dark blue-purple. The bell-shaped blooms are 1½ to 2 inches wide, and the narrow, lepidote leaves are 2 to 3 inches long. Several seedlings and named clones selected for interesting flower color are available. This species grows well in the West, but it is not heat tolerant. Tall, hardy to –5° F.

R. carolinianum

The Carolina rhododendron is a native American species from the East. The pink, funnel-shaped flowers are 1½ inches wide and appear in midseason. Occasionally, white flowers are produced. The growth habit is rounded and compact, and the lepidote leaves range in length from 3 to 4 inches. It grows in sun and does well on both the East and West coasts, but it cannot tolerate the heat of the southern part of the Southeast. Medium, hardy to –25° F.

R. catawbiense

This native of eastern North America has cup-shaped, purplish red flowers, 2½ inches wide, borne in large trusses. The growth habit varies from compact to upright spreading. It is very cold hardy but does not tolerate heat reliably. Several white forms are available, such as 'Catalgla'. Medium to tall, hardy to –25° F.

R. chapmanii and R. minus

These two species are often classified by botanists as varieties of the Carolina rhododendron. Both have pink flowers and lepidote leaves. Both are more heat tolerant than *R. carolinianum* and more open in their habit of growth. Medium, hardy to –15° F.

R. fortunei

This is one of the finest of the rhododendrons from China. The fragrant flowers are white to pale pink, 3 to 4 inches wide, and borne in a large truss. This is a vigorous, large-growing plant with an upright, open habit. The foliage (dark green leaves, 6 to 8 inches long) is attractive and rarely troubled by pests. The plant is often too large for the small garden, but it is excellent when a large, beautiful plant is required. It is one of the common parents, along with *R. decorum*, in developing the Dexter hybrids and others. Tall, hardy to –15° F.

R. keiskei

This species from Japan has several different forms. The dwarf and compact forms are desirable. The small, pale yellow flowers appear early. Blooms are 1½ inches wide and are borne in small trusses. The lepidote leaves are small, 2 to 3 inches long, and the new growth may be bronze-brown. 'Cordifolia' and 'Yaku Fairy' are dwarf forms and compact. Both are excellent for a rock garden or as edging or border plants. Dwarf to low, hardy to –5° F.

Rhododendron mucronulatum

Rhododendron yakushimanum

R. maximum

This large plant is native to eastern North America. Flower buds are pinkish, opening to shades of white, pink, or rose. Blooms are 1½ inches wide and appear late in the season, after the new growth develops. The habit of growth is open and upright. The plant is heat tolerant and is commonly used as a background plant in the East. Tall, hardy to −25° F.

R. moupinense

This beautiful, early-flowering species is native to China. The fragrant, funnel-shaped flowers vary from white to pale pink, with rose-purple spots, and are 2 inches wide. The lepidote leaves are 1½ inches long, and new growth is a bright bronze-red. Growth habit is open and spreading. It is an excellent plant for the West. The flowers need protection from frosts. Low, hardy to 0° F.

R. mucronulatum

A deciduous species native to China and Korea, this is often called an azalea but is classified as a rhododendron because of the small scales on the undersides of the leaves. The purplish pink flowers, 1¾ inches wide, appear along the sides of the stems before the leaves emerge. Because they appear so early, the blooms are susceptible to damage by late frost. Leaves are lance shaped and 4 inches long, and the growth habit is open and upright; heavy shearing increases the amount of bloom and the plant's compactness. This species often blooms at the same time as forsythia, making a striking color combination. 'Cornell Pink' is a clear, light pink selection. Medium, hardy to −25° F.

R. racemosum

This attractive plant from China blooms in early spring. The small, white to pink flowers are 1 inch wide and appear alongside the branches and in small clusters at the stem tips. Leaves are tiny, 1 inch to 2 inches long, lepidote, and blue-green. Available forms vary in growth habit and flower color. This species is frequently used in hybridizing. Low to medium, hardy to −5° F.

R. russatum

The habit of this species is upright and open. The wide funnel-form flowers are ¾ inch long, purple, deep blue, pink, or rose, 4 to 10 to a truss. The leaves are dark green with a dense covering of rust-colored scales on the underneath. Low, hardy to −15° F.

R. yakushimanum

This low, compact plant from the Yakushima Island of Japan is considered one of the best species. The bell-shaped flowers are pink in bud, and they open to white or pale pink, 1¾ inches wide. The new leaves are covered with a soft whitish down. Tan to brown indumentum clothes the lower leaf surfaces. As the small leaves mature to their full size (3 to 4 inches), the whitish down is lost on the top of the leaf. The growth habit is rounded and compact. The plant is cold hardy but does not tolerate heat. A popular species and the parent of many new hybrids. Dwarf to low, hardy to −20° F.

R. yunnanense

This is a beautiful free-flowering shrub from the Yunnan Province of China. The flowers vary from white to pink and are sometimes spotted with red. Blooms are 1½ inches wide and appear in profusion. The lepidote leaves are ½ inch to 3 inches long. The plant is evergreen to semideciduous. This is a superb plant in the West and a must for every rhododendron lover's garden. Unfortunately, it is not much grown in the East, but it can be tried in protected areas in the Southeast. Medium to tall, hardy to 0° F.

Rhododendron aurigeranum

Rhododendron zoelleri

Vireya Rhododendrons

Vireya rhododendrons, often called Malaysian rhododendrons, are tropical species and hybrids of rhododendrons mostly native to New Guinea. The plants cannot tolerate frost and perform best at mild temperatures (45° F and above). They grow the year around in their native habitat. Some of the Vireya species plants are epiphytes, meaning that they grow supported on the limbs of other plants, but they still require light and a loose soil medium.

These plants are often grown outdoors in southern California and are used as container plants for the home or greenhouse in colder areas. The soil medium should be acid and loose and well drained. A good mix is 1 part pine bark (¼ inch size), 1 part peat moss, and 1 part perlite. Plants tend to be leggy. They respond well to frequent pruning and light fertilization.

The flower is very firm, almost to the point of appearing waxed or artificial. Over 160 species of Vireyas have been reported. The following are generally available and respond well to container culture.

R. aurigeranum

Large, funnel-shaped flowers open orange-yellow, then change to yellow. Blooms are 3 inches long, and are carried in trusses of six to eight flowers. The leaves are 3 to 4 inches long, and grow in whorls of five.

R. brookeanum

This is a vigorous plant with slightly fragrant flowers. The funnel-shaped blooms are orange tinged with pink and 2 to 3 inches long. The leaves are very large, 4 to 10 inches long.

R. jasminiflorum

This species has fragrant, tubular, white flowers flushed with pink. The flowers are 1½ inches long and borne in trusses of five to eight blooms. The glossy, dark green leaves are 1 to 2 inches long.

R. javanicum

The large, yellow, funnel-shaped flowers have a reddish or pink tube and pink throat, 2 inches long. The leaves, 1 to 2½ inches long, are in whorls of five to seven.

R. laetum

The large, broad, funnel-shaped flowers are deep yellow blushed with red or orange. The blooms are 2½ to 3 inches long and slightly fragrant. The glossy, dark green leaves are 2 to 3½ inches long.

R. zoelleri

This species has large flowers, usually yellow to orange flushed with pink. The flowers are funnel-shaped, 2½ to 3 inches long, often fragrant, and in trusses of five to eight blooms. The leaves are 3 to 5 inches long, in whorls of four to five.

AZALEAS

Azaleas are divided into four major sections: evergreen hybrids, evergreen species, deciduous hybrids, and deciduous species. The evergreen azaleas are further divided into groups, such as the Belgian Indian hybrids.

Plant Heights

The azaleas described in this section are listed as dwarf, low, medium, or tall.
Dwarf: under 2 feet
Low: 2 to 4 feet
Medium: 4 to 6 feet
Tall: over 6 feet

The bloom seasons can vary by a month or more, depending on the climate. Adapt to your area the season-of-bloom guidelines in the descriptions that follow. In areas with very mild weather, early-blooming plants may begin flowering by the end of February. In cold climates, blooming seasons will be considerably delayed.
Early: late March to early April
Midseason: late April to late May
Late: June to July

Easter Parade

Redwing

Evergreen Azalea Hybrids

Many of the most popular evergreen azalea hybrids are derived from species native to eastern Asia. By custom, the groups of evergreen azalea hybrids are arranged, as shown in the list that follows, according to the order in which they were introduced to this country.

Belgian Indian and Rutherford hybrids

Development of the Belgian Indian, or Belgian, hybrids began in the early 1800s in Europe, mainly Belgium and England. Plants introduced from Japan and China were the ancestors of today's Belgian hybrids. The Sims azalea (*R. simsii*) from China was especially important in the early development of this beautiful group of azaleas. The tender Belgian hybrids were used as greenhouse and indoor plants in Europe. By the early 1840s, the Belgian Indian hybrids, or Indica azaleas as they were called in Europe, had arrived in the United States. They were first introduced in Massachusetts, where they were grown in conservatories and greenhouses. The Rutherford hybrids were first developed in 1929 and are the American equivalent of the Belgian Indian hybrids. Other American Belgian hybrids have been bred mainly in the West and include the Brooks, Gold Cup, Kerrigan, and Whitewater hybrids. Nuccio's Nursery has also introduced a number of Belgian hybrids. Hybridization of these spectacular evergreen azaleas continues, with the main emphasis on developing greenhouse plants for forcing, with semidouble to double ruffled flowers.

The Belgian hybrids are very popular garden and container plants in California and the Deep South. In colder regions of the East, they are grown as greenhouse azaleas for forcing. In the East, many of these plants are not available as outdoor garden stock from garden centers or local nurseries, but they can be purchased as gifts as forced plants. In areas where the plants are too tender to survive the winter outdoors, they can be grown as container plants indoors and moved outdoors in the spring. There is considerable variation in size, flower color, and hardiness among the Belgian Indian and Rutherford hybrids.

Alaska

This popular hybrid is good for forcing. The white ruffled flowers, enhanced by green markings in the throat, are 2 inches wide and semidouble to double. Hardy to 5° F.

Albert and Elizabeth

The white blossom, 3¾ inches wide, has a green throat and is edged in deep pink. A standard greenhouse forcing plant, it also does well as a garden azalea in mild climates. Hardy to 15° F with protection.

California Sunset

This southern California favorite has red flowers, 2½ inches wide, with a pale pink to white margin. Hardy to about 15° F.

Dorothy Gish

This Rutherford hybrid is popular for forcing and exceptionally cold tolerant. The hose-in-hose blooms are 2½ inches wide and appear early midseason. The frilled flowers are a strong reddish orange with a darker blotch. The sport 'White Gish' has snow white flowers. Hardy to 10° F.

Starlight

Delaware Valley White

Easter Parade

This hose-in-hose Mossholder hybrid elegantly complements the Easter season. The 3-inch-wide, ruffled flowers are pale pink with white marbling. 'Easter Bonnet' is similar, with light purplish pink margins and a white throat. 'Sun Valley' of the same group presents a pure white blossom, 2½ inches in width. Hardy to 5° F with protection from cold winds.

Eri
(syn. 'Eric Schäme')

This is a sport of a very old Belgian hybrid, 'Paul Schäme'. The 3-inch-wide double flowers are deep pink with irregular, white margins. A good forcing azalea and garden variety. Hardy to 20° F.

Gay Paree

The frothy white flower edged in dark red is aptly named for its resemblance to a can-can dancer's skirts. Ruffled, hose-in-hose blooms are 3 inches wide. This Kerrigan hybrid is good for forcing. Hardy to 5° F with protection.

Madonna

A Brooks hybrid developed for florists, 'Madonna' is now commonly grown in western gardens. It features a beautiful semidouble, ruffled white flower 3 inches wide. Hardy to 10° F (possibly lower with protection).

Nuccio's Tickled Pink

This beautiful sport of 'Purity' is available in the West. The light pink hose-in-hose flowers, 2½ inches wide, are edged with white. Other Nuccio Belgian hybrids available in the West include 'Nuccio's Garden Party', featuring a deep pink, semidouble flower; 'Nuccio's Masterpiece', a large, white double flower with ruffled petals; and 'Nuccio's Pink Bubbles', a light pink with double, ruffled blossoms. 'Nuccio's Wild Cherry' has vivid red flowers. Hardy to about 15° F.

Pink Ruffles

Sometimes sold as a Southern Indian, it has an upright habit with deep pink, hose-in-hose, ruffled, 3-inch-wide flowers. Tall, hardy to 5° F.

Redwing

This very popular Brooks hybrid, sometimes sold as 'Red Ruffles' or 'Red Bird', has vivid red, ruffled, hose-in-hose flowers that are 2¾ inches wide. It is a good garden and forcing azalea. Hardy to 5° F.

Starlight

A standard in the West, this Kerrigan hybrid makes a striking tub specimen. The semidouble, 3-inch blooms are a soft pink and yellow. Hardy to 10° F (possibly lower with protection).

Southern Indian, or Indica, hybrids

Southern Indian hybrids (sometimes known as Southern Indicas) are generally large plants with large flowers. They are very common in the Deep South. They are more tolerant of hot sun than the Belgian Indians. Most suffer considerable damage at temperatures below 10° F.

Daphne Salmon
(syn. 'Lawsal')

This tall, rangy plant bears intense pink flowers with a darker blotch. Excellent as a tall hedge or screen planting. Hardy to about 5° F.

Delaware Valley White

A white seedling of 'Indica Alba', this is a large, spreading plant. Hardy to about 0° F.

Duchess of Cypress

This variety was introduced by Cypress Gardens. The beautiful light pink, single flowers are marked with white streaks and a white margin, and accented with a reddish blotch. The growth habit is compact and spreading. Hardy to 5° F.

George Lindley Taber

Koromo Shikibu

Formosa

An older variety, 'Formosa' is still a favorite in the South. The flowers are a deep purple-red with a darker blotch. Blooms are 3 inches wide, and flowers appear in early midseason. They blend well with white and pink azaleas, but tend to clash with red or orange varieties. The plant is tall and upright. Hardy to 10° F (often sold outside its hardiness range).

George Lindley Taber

This popular cold-tolerant selection has white to very pale pink flowers, 3½ inches wide, with a light purple-pink flush and a darker blotch. Hardy, for short periods, to 0° F.

Gulfray

This reddish pink variety has an unusual cascading habit that makes it suitable for hanging baskets and tall containers. Planted in the ground, its prostrate habit keeps it very low, which makes it useful in foundation plantings. It grows vigorously and flowers profusely. Discovered in a Mississippi garden, it was just released in 1992. It might be hard to find until stocks are built up. Hardy to about 10° F.

Indica Alba
(syn. *R.* 'Mucronatum', 'Ledifolia Alba')

An old variety found in Japanese gardens more than three hundred years ago. It is often listed as a species (*R. indicum album*) but has never been found in the wild. It is a large shrub bearing single, lightly fragrant, white flowers accented with pale yellow-green dots. Hardy to 0° F.

Koromo Shikibu

The flowers are very distinctive: long, purple-pink, straplike petals, separated to the base, and ½ inch wide and 1½ inches long. This old variety from Japan is often listed as a Kurume. Hardy to 10° F.

Mrs. G. G. Gerbing

This beautiful white sport of 'George Lindley Taber' is not as hardy as its progenitor. It is very popular in the Deep South. Hardy to about 10° F.

Pride of Mobile
(syn. 'Elegans Superba', 'Watermelon Pink')

Very popular in the Deep South and in California, this upright variety has deep purple-pink flowers with a darker blotch. The 2½-inch blooms appear in early midseason. Hardy to 10° F.

Kurume hybrids

Kurume azaleas are among the most popular of the hybrid groups of azaleas. For many years, it was thought that the Kurumes were derived from *R. obtusum*, which turned out to be a very old Japanese hybrid rather than a species. The most important parent of the Kurumes is *R. sataense,* an isolated species from the island of Kyushu in southern Japan.

Kurumes have been grown and revered in Japan for more than three hundred years; they were introduced in California in the early 1900s. Mr. Motozo Sakamoto of Kurume is regarded as the originator of many of the Kurume azaleas in the nineteenth century. In 1915 Mr. Akashi, a nurseryman from Kurume, exhibited 12 varieties of Kurume azaleas at the Panama Pacific Exposition in San Francisco. Following the exhibition, some of the plants were purchased by the Domoto Brothers

Gulfray

Mother's Day

Nursery in California, and in 1917, they obtained the rights to import Kurume azaleas to the United States. Mr. Ernest H. Wilson, a plant explorer for the Arnold Arboretum, also played an important role in introducing Kurume azaleas to the United States. In 1918, Wilson visited Kurume and sent home a selection of azaleas that became known as Wilson's Fifty Kurumes. These were considered the finest azaleas at that time. Unfortunately, all of them are not available in the United States. They all have Japanese names but were also given English names. Varieties such as 'Hinode Giri', 'Coral Bells', and 'Pink Pearl' are still very popular.

Kurumes are hardier than Southern Indians. They are often called dwarfs but will grow into dense, shapely plants, 5 feet or more in height. The small flowers are borne in profusion in early spring and range in color from white to pink, orange, red, and purple. Hardy to −5° to −10° F.

Blaauw's Pink
(syn. 'Glory')
This azalea is often sold under both names. The hose-in-hose flowers are yellow-pink with a darker blotch and are 1¼ inches wide. It has a compact habit.

Bridesmaid
The single flowers are yellowish pink, 1½ inches wide, and have prominent stamens. Its soft color blends well with most other azaleas. The compact plant is an old Domoto hybrid.

Christmas Cheer
A popular Wilson's Fifty, also introduced by Domoto with the Japanese name 'Ima Shojo'. The small, intense red flowers are hose-in-hose, 1¼ inches wide. The plant is dense and upright, often up to 7 feet in height.

Coral Bells
The Japanese name of this very popular plant is 'Kirin', and it is also known as 'Daybreak' and 'Pink Beauty'. The small flowers are strong pink, hose-in-hose, and 1¼ inches wide. The growth habit is compact, and the flowers are borne in profusion.

Hershey's Red
This Kurume hybrid was selected for cold hardiness. The strong red flowers are hose-in-hose and 1½ inches wide. This is an excellent azalea both for the garden and for greenhouse forcing. Other Hershey plants are 'Hershey Orange' and 'Hershey Salmon'. All Hershey azaleas are hardier than most Kurumes.

Hexe
This is an old hybrid developed in Austria. The purple-red flowers are hose-in-hose and 1¾ inches wide. The compact plant blooms in late midseason. Another 'Hexe' from Belgium has a semidouble frilled flower.

Hino Crimson
A Kurume hybrid with small, vivid red flowers that hold their color well. A low to medium plant with red winter foliage.

Hinode Giri
One of the best-known Kurumes, this variety has vivid purple-red flowers, which are best used in mass with pink or white azaleas. Avoid planting 'Hinode Giri' with reddish orange azaleas—the purple tint will clash. Many named sports and hybrids are available.

Hinomayo
This beautiful azalea has single pink flowers on a tall, upright plant. In Japan, the correct name is 'Hinamoyo'.

Mother's Day
The flowers of this variety are vivid red with a faint brown spotting in the blotch. Blooms are hose-in-hose to semidouble and 2 inches wide. The growth habit is compact, with red foliage in the winter.

Nuccio's Jewel Box
An intense pink, hose-in-hose flower, 1½ inches wide. The plant is very dwarf, growing 3 to 5 inches high.

Silver Sword

Vuyk's Scarlet

Orange Cup

This beautiful hybrid has orange to yellowish pink, hose-in-hose flowers and is compact.

Pink Pearl

This fine pink Kurume is the parent of the old pink Kurumes in Japan. The hose-in-hose flowers are an intense pink with a lighter pink center, and are 1¼ inches wide.

Ruth May

From a distance the flowers appear solid pink, but they actually have white stripes and a lighter margin.

Sherwood Red

This is a popular old Kurume. It has a vivid red flower, ¾ inch wide. Prolific blooms cover the upright, compact plants.

Snow

This very popular white was introduced by Domoto Nursery. The pure white, hose-in-hose flowers are 1½ inches wide and have a very light yellow blotch.

The dead flowers often persist and are distracting.

Ward's Ruby

The small, strong red flowers are 1¼ inches wide. They appear in profusion, covering the entire plant. One of the most tender Kurumes, it is easily damaged by cold even in the Northwest.

Kaempferi hybrids

Kaempferi hybrids are crosses of *R. kaempferi* and *R.* 'Malvatica', a clone of unknown parentage from Holland. In Europe, and sometimes in the United States, the Kaempferis are sometimes called the Malvatica hybrids.

Many of the Kaempferi hybrids are vigorous and tall, often growing to 8 feet or more in height, and have an upright growth habit. They make excellent background plantings or single specimens. They can be easily trained to form multiple-trunked, large shrubs or small trees. They are hardy to −10° F.

In colder regions, these azaleas are nearly deciduous in the winter. The flowers are usually single, though some are hose-in-hose. Depending on the cultivar, they bear reddish orange, pink to purple, or white flowers, 1½ to 2½ inches wide. The flowers bloom early to midseason.

Betty

The flowers, vivid purple-pink with a dark throat, are 2 inches wide. The plant is a vigorous grower with a tall, upright habit suitable for training into a multiple-trunked specimen.

Cleopatra

The large flowers are an attractive deep yellow-pink, 2½ inches wide. This tall, upright plant trains easily into a multiple-trunked specimen.

Dorsett

The flowers are deep pink and bloom in the early fall. The plants are medium-sized with an upright habit.

Norma

The 2½-inch-wide flowers are an intense reddish purple with a lighter throat. 'Norma' is an upright plant of medium height that can be used as a multiple-trunked specimen.

Palestrina
(syn. 'Wilhelmina Vuyk')

The white flowers, 2½ inches wide, are marked with a light yellow-green blotch. It is an upright plant that often loses most of its leaves during cold winters but replaces them in spring. This is a very hardy plant.

Silver Sword

A sport of 'Girard's Rose', this new azalea has deep red flowers and variegated leaves with a fine white margin. The leaves turn reddish in the fall, and the margin an attractive pink.

Vuyk's Scarlet

This old, popular azalea from Holland has frilled, deep red flowers 2 inches wide. It is a compact plant.

Stewartstonian

Girard's Hot Shot

Gable hybrids

Joseph B. Gable introduced some of the first hardy evergreen azaleas in the United States. Many of his plants were crosses of *R. yedoense* var. *poukhanense* with *R. kaempferi*. The Gable hybrids are widely accepted and used by other hybridizers. Most Gable hybrids are hardy to −10° F; some can withstand even lower temperatures.

Big Joe

The flowers of this ever-popular Gable selection are a strong purplish pink with a brownish blotch. Blooms are 2½ inches wide and appear in early midseason. A medium, spreading plant.

Caroline Gable

The attractive flowers are vivid red, 1¾ inches wide, and bloom in late midseason. It is a very colorful, very hardy landscape plant.

Herbert

The frilled, hose-in-hose flowers, 1¾ inches wide, are a vivid reddish purple with a darker blotch. They bloom in early midseason. The plant is low to medium with a spreading habit.

James Gable

The hose-in-hose flowers are a deep pink with a darker blotch. They bloom in early midseason. The plant is tall and upright.

Louise Gable

The developer of 'Louise Gable' considered this one of his finest azaleas. The semidouble flowers are deep yellowish pink with a darker blotch, and are 2¼ inches wide. The growth habit is low and dense.

Mildred Mae

The reddish purple, single flowers of this hybrid bloom in early midseason. This medium-sized plant has a compact habit.

Purple Splendor

The reddish purple, hose-in-hose, frilled flowers of this popular variety are 1¾ inches wide. It is frequently used as a parent in hybridizing.

Rose Greeley

One of Gable's long-range plans was to develop a hardy white azalea, and this was the result after 16 years of work. The beautiful white, hose-in-hose flower is accented by a chartreuse blotch. The sweet-scented blossoms are 2½ inches wide, and they bloom early. The plant is hardy, with a low, dense habit.

Rosebud
(syn. 'Gable's Rosebud')

This hybrid has beautiful double flowers that open like rosebuds. The flowers, 1¾ inches wide, are a deep purple-pink. They bloom from midseason to late. The growth habit is low, dense, and spreading. It is considered the best of several different 'Rosebud' azaleas in the trade. 'Lorna' is another pink double azalea with flowers like rosebuds.

Stewartstonian

This attractive plant has brilliant red flowers, 2 inches wide. It is tall and upright, with reddish brown winter foliage.

Girard hybrids

Peter Girard, Sr., a nurseryman from Geneva, Ohio, hybridized azaleas and rhododendrons for over forty years. His evergreen azaleas are noted for their hardiness and compact growth. Girard azaleas were initially developed for the Midwest, but are now grown from coast to coast and in Europe. All are hardy to about −15° F.

Custom White

The large, white flowers are 2½ inches to 3 inches wide and have wavy petals. It is a semiupright plant.

Girard's Border Gem

This sport of 'Girard's Rose' has attractive deep pink flowers, 1½ inches wide. The plant has a dense growth habit and small leaves.

Girard's Hot Shot

The deep reddish orange flowers are marked with dark red spots. The petals are wavy, and the blooms are 2½ inches wide. This low plant has reddish winter foliage. Often sold as 'Hot Shot'.

Garden State Pink

Janet Rhea

Girard's Rose

The deep pink flowers with wavy petals are 2½ inches wide. It is a compact plant with reddish brown winter foliage.

Girard's Variegated Gem

This new sport of 'Girard's Border Gem' has small, elliptical leaves, 1¼ inches long, with an attractive yellowish margin. This neat, compact dwarf plant has deep pink flowers.

Purple Robe

This is a beautiful purple azalea. The hose-in-hose flowers, 2 inches wide, are purple with wavy petals. It has a semi-upright habit and good reddish winter foliage.

Unsurpassable

This is a broad, dense plant bearing deep pink flowers, 2¾ inches wide, with wavy petals.

Linwood hybrids

Dr. Charles Fischer started to develop hardy greenhouse forcing azaleas in Linwood, New Jersey, in 1950. Soon after, Albert Reid took over the project to develop cold-hardy landscape azaleas. The parents include Kurume and Kaempferi hybrids. More than 25 have been introduced, many of which are named for the Garden State. Most are hardy to about −15° F and have a low to medium growth habit.

'Garden State Glow' has strong purplish red, hose-in-hose flowers.

'Garden State Pink' has pink, hose-in-hose blossoms.

'Garden State Red' has vivid purplish red, hose-in-hose flowers.

'Garden State Salmon' has vivid reddish orange, hose-in-hose blossoms.

'Garden State White' has white, hose-in-hose flowers.

Others have the name Linwood. 'Linwood Blush' has light yellow-pink, double hose-in-hose blossoms. 'Linwood Lustre' has white, hose-in-hose blossoms with greenish yellow spots that blend into a dorsal blotch. 'Linwood Lavender' has light purple, semidouble blossoms. 'Linwood Pink Giant' has strong purplish red, hose-in-hose blossoms.

Hardy Gardenia

This is a hardy plant with double white flowers and attractive dark green winter foliage.

Janet Rhea

This variety has unusually striking flowers for a hardy azalea. The hose-in-hose flowers are purple-red with irregular white margins. Blooms are 2½ inches wide. Hardy to −5° F.

Opal

This hybrid has deep pink, single flowers that bloom in the early fall as well as in the spring.

Pride hybrids

Orlando Pride of Butler, Pennsylvania, introduced a number of cold-hardy deciduous and evergreen azaleas and rhododendrons. The evergreen azaleas were usually crosses of *R. kaempferi* with *R. yedoense* var. *poukhanense*. Over sixty were introduced, but many are not available except in private gardens. The following can be found in the Northeast.

'Charles A. Pride' has strong yellowish pink flowers.

'Nadine' is a cold-hardy plant with light pink flowers. It was one of the first Pride hybrids and is the parent of many of the others.

'Pride's Red' has dark red flowers and blooms late.

'Pride's White' is a very hardy white.

'Susan Page' has hose-in-hose, yellowish pink flowers.

'Vickies' has reddish orange blossoms.

'Watermelon' has blooms of a moderate pink.

Shammarello hybrids

Tony Shammarello introduced evergreen azaleas noted for both cold hardiness and good growth habit. All are suitable for general landscape use and are hardy to −15° F.

Ben Morrison

Dayspring

Desiree
This medium-sized plant has frilled, white flowers, 2½ inches wide. It blooms early midseason.

Elsie Lee
A very hardy dwarf plant with light reddish purple, semidouble flowers, it blooms early to early midseason.

Hino-Red
This is a compact plant with early red flowers, 1¾ inches wide. There is no tint of purple in the flowers.

Hino-White
This hardy plant is a good replacement for 'Snow' in colder areas. The plant is compact and spreading, with white flowers 2 inches wide.

Pink Gem
This upright, spreading plant has attractive pink flowers 2 inches wide.

Stanton hybrids
Developed by Ernest Stanton, this group of hardy evergreen azaleas is not generally known. They are low to medium-sized plants, and are hardy to about –15° F.

'Lake Erie' has deep pink flowers.

'Lake Michigan' has purplish pink flowers.

'Lake Superior' has deep purplish pink flowers.

'Shawnee' has reddish orange blossoms; blooms early; and has a tall, upright habit.

Glenn Dale hybrids
The Glenn Dale azaleas are the results of the largest breeding program in the United States, which was instituted by B. Y. Morrison, former director of the United States National Arboretum. The objective was to produce large-flowered azaleas hardy in the Washington, D.C., area. The resulting hybrids range from early- to late-flowering plants and have a wide variety of colors. Over four hundred fifty cultivars were named. The Glenn Dale azaleas are very popular in the East and are grown in other parts of the United States as well. The best sources for many of the varieties are nurseries specializing in azaleas. All are hardy to –10° F.

Ambrosia
The deep yellow-pink flower, changing to a light orange-yellow, is 1½ to 2 inches wide. This early-blooming, broad, upright plant grows to 8 feet.

Ben Morrison
This popular hybrid of the Glenn Dale series was named in Morrison's honor after his death. The spectacular flowers, 2½ inches wide, are deep yellowish pink with an irregular white margin and a purplish red blotch. The white margins are often not pronounced until the plant matures. A different hybrid, 'B. Y. Morrison', has reddish orange blossoms; its flower buds are not as hardy as 'Ben Morrison'.

Boldface
The beautiful, white-centered flowers have a purplish pink margin and a red blotch. The flowers are 3 inches wide and appear midseason. This compact plant grows to 4 feet.

Buccaneer
This is one of the best Glenn Dales. The early-blooming flowers, 2 inches wide, are a vivid reddish orange with a darker upper lobe. The flowers scorch in direct sun, so plants should be placed in partial shade.

Copperman
The beautiful, deep yellow-pink flowers shaded with orange are accented by a dark blotch. The late-blooming flowers are 2¾ inches wide. A compact plant of medium height.

Dayspring
The striking flowers of this top Glenn Dale azalea are 1½ to 2 inches wide, with white centers shading to a light lavender margin. The broad, spreading plant is tall and blooms midseason.

Fashion

Martha Hitchcock

Delos

The double flowers are light purple-pink, 2½ inches wide, and bloom midseason. The plant is erect and spreading in habit. The heavy flowers may break the arching branches.

Dream

The vivid purplish pink, frilled flowers, 2¾ inches wide, are accented with a dark blotch. 'Dream' has an upright, spreading habit and blooms early.

Fashion

This favorite variety has hose-in-hose flowers of a deep yellow-pink with a purplish red blotch. The flowers are 2 inches wide. The tall, spreading plant blooms early.

Festive

The flowers appear pale pink, but they are actually white with purple-red stripes and speckles. The flowers are 2 to 2½ inches wide. 'Festive' is tall and spreading, and blooms early.

Glacier

This is one of the best Glenn Dales. The early flowers are white faintly tinged with green, 2½ to 3 inches wide. The leaves are a dark, lustrous green and stay green in the winter. The upright spreading plant is tall.

Glamour

This is a beautiful, early-blooming azalea with vivid purplish pink flowers, 2 to 3 inches wide. The plant is medium and spreading.

Helen Close

This is a beautiful midseason white flower, 2½ inches wide, with a pale yellow blotch. To create a white azalea garden, you could start with the Kurume 'Snow', followed by 'Glacier', 'Treasure', and then 'Helen Close'.

Martha Hitchcock

This is a real favorite. The beautiful white flowers are edged in purplish red. Blooms are 3 inches wide, appearing early midseason. The medium, spreading plant occasionally produces

shoots with solid purplish red flowers. For an interesting effect, leave these on the plant until the blooms have faded, then prune them off.

Refrain

This azalea has interesting variations in the flower. The typical hose-in-hose flower, 2 inches wide, is white suffused with lavender, edged with white, and marked with pink stripes and a distinct blotch of purplish pink dots. Some flowers show no white and are a pale lavender-pink throughout, with a blotch. The plant is tall and blooms early.

Treasure

This beautiful, near-white azalea is a good substitute for 'Indica Alba'. The pastel pink buds open to white with a very pale pink margin and pink dots in the blotch. The flowers are 3 to 4 inches wide. It is a tall, spreading plant.

Back Acres hybrids

B. Y. Morrison, who also developed the Glenn Dale hybrids, developed the Back Acres hybrids after he retired to Mississippi. They are noted for their heat tolerance and large, substantial flowers, and are generally midseason bloomers. The medium-sized plants are cold hardy to –10° F, but the flower buds are not as cold resistant as those of the Glenn Dale hybrids. The following plants are more readily available than many others, which are only available from azalea nurseries.

Debonaire

The flowers of this variety are a beautiful cool color for warm weather. The 3-inch-wide flowers are a vivid pink with a lighter, greenish center and a deep pink margin. The plant grows slowly and remains low.

Elise Norfleet

The showy, pastel pink flowers are edged in vivid red with darker dots in the blotch. The flower color varies on young plants.

Betty Ann Voss

Nancy of Robinhill

Margaret Douglas

This very popular plant has spectacular 3-inch-wide flowers, light pink in the center with a wide margin of yellowish pink. It is a medium, spreading plant.

Marian Lee

The 3-inch-wide flowers have a white, purple-tinged center and a red border.

Red Slipper

This popular midseason azalea has flowers, 3 inches wide, that are brilliant purplish red accented with carmine dots in the blotch.

White Jade

The 3-inch-wide, ruffled flowers are white flushed with pale green on the upper lobe. This azalea is effective with the stronger colors of the other Back Acre azaleas.

Robin Hill hybrids

Robert Gartrell developed these hardy, late-blooming azaleas, which have many characteristics of the Satsuki hybrids. In general, the plants are as hardy as the Satsuki and Kurume azaleas. The plants average 3 to 5 feet in height, and the growth rate varies from slow to medium. Flowers range from single, to hose-in-hose, to full double, and may be shades of white, pink, purple, and red. Sixty-nine cultivars have been named. They are late bloomers.

Betty Anne Voss

This beautiful flower has buds that open like a rose. The double hose-in-hose flowers are vivid to pale purplish pink and 3 inches wide. This is a low, compact plant.

Conversation Piece

The 3½-inch-wide flowers have wavy petals and are extremely variable in color. The flowers are basically white with a spotted blotch of purplish red. Some flowers are marked with wedges of solid shades of purplish pink;

some colored flowers have a lighter margin. One plant may have the complete range of color patterns. This is a low, mounding plant.

Lady Robin

This low to medium variety has interesting variable white flowers, 3 inches wide, with wedges and stripes of vivid purplish red.

Mrs. Emil Hager

This dwarf plant has semidouble to double hose-in-hose flowers. Blooms are deep purple-pink and 2¾ inches wide.

Nancy of Robinhill

This low-growing azalea has semidouble to double flowers, 3½ inches wide, that are a light purple-pink with a light red blotch.

Sara Holden

This mounding plant has interesting 2½-inch-wide, white flowers. The variable flowers often have five or six lobes, adding interest to the color pattern.

Turk's Cap

This plant is well named. The flower petals are curved downward in much the same way as the petals of a lily. The blooms of 'Turk's Cap' are reddish and 3½ inches wide.

Watchet

The ruffled flowers, 3½ inches wide, are a beautiful pink with a pale greenish white throat. This plant blooms again in the fall in the South.

Wee Willie

This is a neat, compact plant. The 2½-inch-wide, light purple-pink flowers appear extra large on this dwarf azalea.

Satsuki hybrids

Satsuki azaleas are from Japan, though recent hybrids have been developed in the United States. They are very popular as bonsai plants, and are also excellent landscape plants noted for their late flowers. The Satsuki azaleas sport freely and are variable in flower color and plant habit. Some have a spreading, low-growing

Balsaminaeflorum

Gumpo Pink

habit; others attain medium height in 10 to 15 years. The plants are mostly rounded in shape, with a twiggy, compact growth; a few are pendulous. They are hardy to about –5° F. Because of the late and often large flowers, the plants need protection from the afternoon sun. Over six hundred Satsukis are grown in the United States. It is impossible to list all of the many fine hybrids within this group; the following will whet your appetite.

Balsaminaeflorum

A beautiful double form of *R. indicum*, this is a low, mounding plant with deep yellowish pink to reddish orange flowers, 1½ inches wide. The flowers are very double with many petals, and they open like a rosebud. An excellent specimen azalea and also good for planting in front of larger shrubs.

Bunka
(syn. 'Bunkwa')

The 4-inch-wide flowers have six rounded lobes. The flowers may be white with pink flecks or solid colors from light to deep pink.

Eikan
(syn. 'Eikwan')

This fine variable azalea has large, rounded flowers, 3 to 4 inches wide, often with six to nine lobes. The base color is white with many variations of stripes and solid colors of deep pink to deep yellowish pink. The plant is vigorous and spreading. The hybrid 'Linda R.' is a beautiful yellowish pink sport.

Flame Creeper

This low, creeping form of *R. indicum* is excellent for trailing over walls, as a ground cover, or as a basket plant. The 2-inch-wide flowers are reddish orange.

Gumpo
(syn. 'Gunpo')

The Gumpo group includes some of the best-known Satsukis in the United States. They are beautiful, low-mounding, late-blooming plants. 'Gumpo White' has beautiful, large (3 inches wide) white flowers with wavy overlapping petals and occasional purple flecks. 'Gumpo Pink' has pale to light pink flowers with wavy petals. 'Gumpo Fancy' has beautiful pink

flowers, 3 inches wide, with a distinct white margin. 'Dwarf Gumpo' is a dwarf sport of 'Gumpo', bearing white flowers, 1½ inches wide, with pink stripes and flecks. 'Mini Gumpo' is a sport of 'Dwarf Gumpo', with white to pink flowers, 1¼ inches wide, and tiny leaves ¼ to ⅜ inch long.

Keisetsu

The attractive variegated leaves are dark green with small yellowish blotches and lines. The 3-inch-wide flowers are a strong red with a light pink to nearly white center. Occasionally, the margins are deep pink. The foliage of this plant may provide an attractive contrast.

Kinsai

The very irregular flower has separate, long, narrow petals, 1½ to 2 inches long. The deep orange flowers seem spiderlike. This low, spreading plant with narrow leaves, 1 to 1¼ inches long, is popular for bonsai.

Macrantha

A selection of *R. indicum* often listed as a species *R. macrantha*, this is a compact, mounding shrub of medium height with dark green, elliptical leaves, 1½ to 2 inches long. The late-blooming flowers are reddish orange and 2½ inches wide. Other forms include 'Macrantha Pink', 'Macrantha Double', and 'Macrantha Dwarf'.

Rukizon
(syn. 'Kazan')

This interesting compact plant has broad, dark green, glossy leaves, ½ inch or less in length. The leaves are often described as heart-shaped. The flowers are small for a Satsuki, only 1½ to 2 inches wide, and are light red with a dotted blotch. This is a low, mounding plant.

Shinnyo-No-Tsuki

This spectacular variety has large, 3½-inch-wide flowers with overlapping lobes. The blooms may be solid colors or white with wedges or stripes of vivid purplish red or a wide, purplish red margin. This very popular plant is the parent of many Satsuki hybrids.

Shinnyo-No-Tsuki

Joseph Hill

Shira Fuji

This beautiful plant is noted for its variegated leaves. The flower color varies from solid purple to solid white. Occasionally, the flowers are white with stripes and blushes of purplish pink. The plant suffers leaf damage below 10° F.

Wakaebisu

This hybrid has beautiful, deep yellowish pink, hose-in-hose flowers, 2 to 2½ inches wide, with deep pink dots in the blotch. This is a popular landscape and container or bonsai plant. The plant is hardy to 5° F.

Warai Jishi

An upright, mounding plant with irregular double flowers. The flowers are deep purple-pink with widely spaced, pointed lobes, 2½ inches wide.

Yachiyo Red

This low, compact plant was introduced from Japan. The name is confusing because the colorful flowers are not red but are white with light pink blotches, stripes, or wedges. Sometimes,

the blossoms are solid shades of light pink. It is a good dwarf plant for containers or landscape.

Pericat hybrids

Developed by Alphonse Pericat for greenhouse forcing, these hybrids are hardy outdoors in many areas. Most of the Pericats are as hardy as Kurumes. The following are generally available.

Dawn

The hose-in-hose, purplish pink flower has a white to light pink center and is 2½ inches wide. The plant has a dense and spreading habit.

Hampton Beauty

The dark, candy-striped buds open to a light pink, 2-inch blossom. The medium, spreading plants bloom early to early midseason.

North Tisbury hybrids

Polly Hill of Martha's Vineyard, Massachusetts, began to propagate seed and cuttings of azaleas sent to her from Japan in the 1960s. Some are seedlings of *R. nakaharai* and others are crosses of *R. nakaharai* with other hybrids. Some of the North Tisbury hybrids include cuttings of Satsuki azaleas that she has named in the United States. Many are dwarf, spreading plants. The North Tisbury hybrids are excellent as ground covers, for trailing over walls, and for hanging baskets.

Alexander

This low, creeping, irregular, mounding plant is usually less than 12 inches tall, except in the Deep South. The flowers are 2½ inches wide, deep reddish orange with a darker blotch, and late blooming.

Hotline

This is a seedling of a dwarf 'Gumpo'. The late-blooming flowers, 3 inches wide, are a vivid purplish red with a deep red blotch.

Jeff Hill

The 2-inch-wide flowers of this low plant are deep pink with a red blotch and have wavy petals.

Joseph Hill

This dwarf, creeping plant has vivid red flowers, 2¼ inches wide, with wavy petals.

Late Love

This is a dwarf, creeping plant with bright pink flowers, 2¼ inches wide, with a purplish red blotch. Flowers appear very late.

Libby

This seedling of *R. kaempferi* has light purple-pink flowers, 1¾ inches wide, with wavy petals. The compact, upright plant blooms midseason.

Michael Hill

This dwarf, spreading plant grows 18 inches high and 48 inches wide in 10 years. The late-blooming flowers are intense to medium pink with a purplish red blotch. Blooms are 2¾ inches wide, and the petals are frilled. It is a good ground

Pink pancake

Flower girl

cover and is beautiful when allowed to trail down over a wall. Hardy to –10° F.

Mount Seven Star

This beautiful selection of *R. nakaharai* was grown from seeds collected on Mt. Seven Stars in Taiwan. The low, creeping plant remains less than 12 inches high. The vivid red flowers are 2 inches wide with a faint blotch and wavy petals. This late bloomer is an excellent rock garden plant.

Pink Pancake

This low, creeping plant is less than 12 inches high. The wavy-petaled flowers are bright pink with purplish red dots in the blotch.

Winter Green

This plant forms a circular mound, growing to about 12 inches high and 36 inches wide in 10 years. The deep pink flowers are 2 inches across and blossom in midseason to late season.

Beltsville dwarfs

The Beltsville dwarfs are a group of azaleas selected over 25 years ago from a breeding program by the Department of Agriculture at Beltsville, Maryland. These slow-growing plants are ideal for small gardens and as border plants. They are excellent for growing in containers and for bonsai. They flower in early spring but can be easily forced for late-winter bloom. Many Beltsville hybrids are true genetic dwarfs: a six-year-old plant is usually 6 to 8 inches tall and as wide or wider (sometimes as much as three times) than it is high. Hardy to –10° F.

Boutonniere

The small, white, hose-in-hose flowers, 1½ inches wide, have a pale yellow throat. Dwarf, usually wider than high.

Flower Girl

The dark pink, single flowers are 1½ inches wide and are borne profusely. Twice as wide as high.

Pink Elf

The light yellow-pink, hose-in-hose flowers are 1¼ inches wide and completely cover the plant. Dwarf, about three times as wide as high.

Purple Cushion

The single, purple flowers are 1½ inches wide. Dwarf, usually twice as wide as high.

Salmon Elf

The hose-in-hose, yellowish pink flowers are 1¼ inches wide. A mature plant 25 years old is less than 30 inches high. Dwarf, usually as wide as high.

Snowdrop

The white, hose-in-hose flowers are 1¼ inches wide. Dwarf, usually three times as wide as high.

White Doll

The white, single flowers are 1¼ inches wide and cover the entire plant in spring. Dwarf, usually twice as wide as high.

Greenwood hybrids

Greenwoods are a new group of evergreen azaleas for the Northwest developed by Bill Gutormsen of Oregon. These hybrids range from low to medium in height and overall size. The Greenwood hybrids are as hardy as the Glenn Dales and are well suited for the East and the West. Hardy to –10° F.

Can Can

The purplish, frilled flowers are semidouble to double, 3 inches wide, and late blooming. The plant is low, rounded, and compact.

Genie Magic

This low, compact, and broadly rounded plant blooms in early spring. The medium red, hose-in-hose flowers are 2 inches wide and cover the entire plant.

Greenwood Rosebud

The beautiful roselike flowers are deep purple-pink, double hose-in-hose, and 2¾ inches wide. The plant is low and compact.

Tina

Fascination

Orange Sherbet

This low, spreading plant has double, vivid red flowers, 2¾ inches wide, in midseason.

Silver Streak

This is a variegated sport of 'Deep Purple', with white margins and light mottling on the leaves. The deep purple-red, hose-in-hose flowers are 2¼ inches wide and bloom early.

Tina

The early-blooming, hose-in-hose flowers are 1 inch wide and a vivid purple-red. Its low, compact, and rounded habit makes this a good border plant.

August Kehr hybrids

August Kehr is a retired geneticist and an active hybridizer of both rhododendrons and azaleas. There are not many August Kehr hybrids, but they are worth seeking out. They are excellent double-flowering azaleas. Hardy to –5° F.

Anna Kehr

Each lovely purple-pink flower, 1¾ inches wide, has 40 wavy petals. The upright plant is quite compact.

Great Expectations

A recent introduction, this low plant has vivid reddish orange, double flowers, 2 inches wide.

Kehr's White Rosebud

The blooms look like white rosebuds. The beautiful double flower, 1¾ to 2 inches wide, has about 40 petals.

Harris hybrids

Developed by James Harris of Georgia, these hybrids are just becoming known throughout the country. Over thirty plants have been introduced. Nearly all should be hardy to –5° F.

Ellie Harris

A beautiful light pink, hose-in-hose flower. The blooms are 2 inches wide and appear early midseason. It is a low shrub (growing to 3 feet in 10 years) and has a slightly spreading habit. Hardy to –5° F.

Fascination

The beautiful large flower, 4½ inches wide, has a pale pink center with a red border. The blooms are fragrant, and the rounded petals give the flower a starlike appearance.

Parfait

The 2-inch-wide flower is pink with a white center marked with a red-dotted blotch. Blooms are slightly fragrant and appear early midseason. The low to medium shrub has a rounded habit. Hardy to about –10° F.

Pink Cascade

The plant has a cascading, spreading habit and is an excellent plant for hanging baskets or as ground cover. The flowers are 2 inches wide and deep yellow-pink with a red blotch.

Virginia Royalty hybrids

George Ring bred this series in Fairfax, Virginia, to have strong root systems and to be hardy to at least –5° F. All are very floriferous. They were just introduced in the 1980s, so they may be difficult to locate for a little while.

'Virginia Baroness' bears large, white, hose-in-hose flowers in midseason on a broad shrub that can spread to 4 feet.

'Virginia Prince' has light pink flowers on an upright shrub.

'Virginia Queen' bears, in midseason, light pink flowers that can be 4 inches across. It has a broad, spreading habit.

Schroeder hybrids

Developed in the 1970s by Dr. Henry Schroeder especially for cold hardiness, this group is also known for its attractive foliage and compact growth habit. All are hardy to about –15° F.

'Mrs. Henry Schroeder' bears double, deep pink flowers about 2 inches across. 'Purple Pride'

Rhododendron macrosepalum *var.* linearifolium

Rhododendron nakaharai

has ruffled, reddish purple flowers, 2½ inches across. 'Scarlet Frost' has red flowers and especially shiny foliage. 'Schroeder's White Glory' bears small (1½ inches), white, hose-in-hose flowers with pink edges.

Evergreen Azalea Species

Most of the evergreen azalea species are native to Japan, where many have been grown for over three hundred years. The following are some of the most important species grown as garden plants and used for hybridizing.

R. kaempferi (Kaempfer or torch azalea)

Good for mass plantings, this large shrub is usually evergreen but may be deciduous in cooler climates. Flowers range from yellowish pink to reddish orange. A rare white form also exists. Hardy to –5° F.

R. kiusianum (Kyushu azalea)

This dwarf species is from the mountains of Japan. The flowers are usually purplish pink, but a white form is frequently grown, and other colored selections are being introduced. 'Benichidori' is light reddish orange. The plant is often deciduous in cooler areas. Hardy to –10° F.

R. macrosepalum var. linearifolium (Spider azalea)

An unusual plant with narrow, straplike leaves, 3 inches long and ½ inch wide. The flowers are violet, and long and linear like the leaves. It is of garden origin and has been known in Japan for over three hundred years by the name 'Seigai'. It is a very striking accent plant with attractive fall foliage color. Hardy to 5° F.

R. nakaharai

This compact dwarf plant is native to the mountains of Korea. The deep pink to reddish orange flowers bloom midseason. Hardy to –5° F.

R. obtusum (Obtusum azalea)

Introduced from an old garden in China, the original plant came from Japan. The flowers are pink. It is no longer considered a species, since it was not found in the wild. It was originally thought to be the parent of the Kurume hybrids developed in Japan over three hundred years ago. However, it has been determined that the original parent of the Kurumes is a rare species, *R. sataense*, from Kyushu Island of Japan. Hardy to –5° F.

R. serpyllifolium (Wildthyme azalea)

This low, dense, and spreading plant is native to Japan and is a good bonsai subject. The small, pink flowers are ¾ inch wide, and the leaves are ¼ to ¾ inch long. A white form, *R. albiflorum,* is very popular. The tiny flowers look like snowflakes on the plant in early spring. Hardy to –10° F.

Deciduous Azalea Hybrids

The parents of most modern deciduous azalea hybrids were species introduced to western Europe and England from the late 1600s to the early 1800s. Some of these early introductions included the species *R. viscosum* (swamp azalea), *R. periclymanoides* (pinxterbloom azalea), *R. alendulaceum* (flame azalea), *R. molle* (Chinese azalea), and *R. japonicum*. The Ghent and Mollis hybrids came from these early plant introductions.

    The development of the Ghent azaleas began in the early 1800s in Ghent, Belgium, when

Cecile

Homebush

P. Mortier crossed flame azaleas with pinxterbloom azaleas. The Mollis and Ghent hybrids have been generally replaced by the Knap Hill, Exbury, and Ilam hybrids.

In 1870 Anthony Waterer and his son worked to improve the Ghents by crossing them with the Chinese azalea and other species. The resulting crosses were named after the Waterers' Knap Hill nursery in England. In 1922 Lionel de Rothschild of Exbury, England, obtained several Knap Hill seedlings and bred the Exbury hybrids. The Ilam hybrids were developed by Edgar Stead at the Ilam Estate in Christ Church, New Zealand. He began by crossing Knap Hill azaleas and several North American native species. His work was continued by Dr. J. S. Yeates. The Ilam, Knap Hill, and Exbury hybrids were reported to be heat tolerant. However, heat tolerance of these groups is variable and depends on the particular cultivar.

A recent group, the Windsor hybrids, has been selected from seedlings by Sir Eric Savill in the Savill Gardens, Windsor Great Park, England.

In the early 1980s, the University of Minnesota released the Northern Lights series. These deciduous azaleas are very hardy—to at least −35° F—and also perform well in more moderate climates.

The large flowers of deciduous azaleas vary from white to yellow, pink, orange, or red. There are numerous named cultivars and seedlings available in the cool regions of the East and West. Most are cold tolerant but are less well adapted to warm regions. Over five hundred named varieties of deciduous azaleas have been introduced.

Balzac
This Exbury hybrid has fragrant, reddish orange flowers, 2 inches wide. The petals are pointed and widely spaced, giving the flowers a starlike appearance.

Berry Rose
The large, fragrant flowers of this Exbury hybrid are reddish orange flushed with pink and marked with a yellow blotch. The plant is a vigorous grower, and the new leaves are reddish.

Brazil
This Exbury hybrid has frilled, reddish orange flowers. The blooms are 1¾ inches wide, and are borne in large trusses.

Buzzard
This Knap Hill hybrid has beautiful, fragrant, yellow flowers tinged pink.

Cecile
This very popular Exbury variety has deep pink flower buds opening to deep yellow-pink with a yellow blotch.

Coccinea Speciosa
This is a very old Ghent hybrid and one of the best of the old varieties. The 2½-inch-wide flowers are a reddish orange accented with a yellowish blotch.

Daviesi
This is another old Ghent hybrid. The fragrant flowers are very pale yellow fading to white with a showy yellow blotch. The tall, upright plant is heat tolerant.

Gibraltar
This Exbury hybrid is one of the best known deciduous azaleas. The frilled flowers are a vivid orange tinged with red, 2½ inches wide, and borne in a large truss. It is heat tolerant in warmer climates as long as it is well watered and protected from hot afternoon sun.

Golden Sunset
This Exbury hybrid has large, attractive flowers that are reddish orange in bud, opening to yellow with a distinct orange blotch.

Graciosa
This old Occidentale hybrid was developed in Holland. The fragrant, pale orange-yellow flower is accented with a yellowish blotch. It grows best in the West and needs partial shade.

Homebush
Interesting large, spherical trusses are a feature of this Knap Hill azalea. The deep pink flowers are hose-in-hose and 1¼ inches wide. One of the most popular of the double-flowered azaleas.

Narcissiflora

Rhododendron atlanticum

Hotspur

This popular hybrid has large, reddish orange, 4-inch-wide flowers highlighted with a yellow blotch. The new foliage has a reddish tint. There are several named sister seedlings of 'Hotspur': 'Hotspur Orange', 'Hotspur Red', and 'Hotspur Yellow'.

Kathleen

This Exbury hybrid has beautiful pale orange flowers blushed with pink and a deep orange blotch.

Klondyke

This superb Exbury hybrid has flower buds that are reddish orange and yellow, opening to a vivid yellow with a darker blotch. New leaves have a reddish tint.

Marion Merriman

This popular Knap Hill hybrid has wide, flattened flowers. The bright yellow flowers are flushed with orange and marked with a vivid orange blotch.

Mount Saint Helen (syn. 'Girard's Mount Saint Helen')

The fragrant flower is pink and yellow with a large reddish orange blotch. The petals are wavy, and the growth habit is upright.

Narcissiflora

This is an old but still popular Ghent hybrid. The hose-in-hose, pale yellow flowers are a delight in any garden, and its fragrance and heat tolerance are additional attractions.

Oxydol

This fine white Exbury hybrid blends well with yellow, pink, and orange-to-red azaleas. The large, white, 2½-inch-wide flowers have a distinctive yellow blotch.

Persian Melon

An Ilam hybrid, this plant produces trusses of orange-yellow flowers.

Pink Lights

This Northern Lights hybrid has moderate pink, fragrant flowers with orange spots.

Rosy Lights

This is another Northern Lights release with vivid purplish red blossoms. It grows to a spreading 4 feet high and will survive winters to –45° F.

Strawberry Ice

The name of this choice Exbury hybrid is very descriptive. The flowers are light yellow-pink tinged with orange and marked with a large yellow blotch.

White Lights

The rose-colored buds of this Northern Lights release open pale pink to white. It is fragrant and hardy to –45° F. The shrub grows slowly to 3 to 4 feet high.

Deciduous Azalea Species

Native to Europe, Asia, and North America, deciduous azalea species include some of the most common species used in gardens.

R. alabamense (Alabama azalea)

This is a native of Alabama and Georgia. Its fragrant, white flowers, 1½ inches wide, have a showy yellow blotch. They bloom early midseason. Pinkish hybrid forms are often available as seedlings. Hardy to –15° F.

R. arborescens (Sweet azalea)

The fragrant, white flowers, 1½ inches wide, have contrasting red stamens. Flowers bloom midseason to late. This species is native to the Southeast. Hardy to –15° F.

Rhododendron austrinum

Rhododendron occidentale

Rhododendron prunifolium

R. atlanticum
(Coastal azalea)

A native of the East Coast, this species bears white to pale pink, fragrant flowers, 1½ inches wide, with a yellow blotch. It is a low to medium plant that spreads by stolons. Hardy to –15° F.

R. austrinum
(Florida azalea)

This species is native to the lower regions of the Southeast. The fragrant, yellow flowers, 1½ inches wide, are often tinged with pink. Early blooming. Hardy to –10° F.

R. bakeri
(Cumberland azalea)

A variable shrub, usually ranging from 2 to 5 feet in height, but sometimes growing taller. It is native to Kentucky, Tennessee, northern Georgia, Alabama, and North Carolina. The flowers are 1½

inches wide, reddish orange to orange, and usually marked with an orange blotch. Blooms appear late midseason, two to four weeks after the flame azalea. Hardy to –20° F.

R. calendulaceum
(Flame azalea)

This species is native to the Appalachian Mountains. The flowers are large, 1¾ to 2½ inches wide, and are yellow to reddish orange. There are two forms—one a midseason bloomer and the other a late bloomer. Hardy to –25° F.

R. canescens (Florida pinxterbloom azalea)

The most common native species of the Southeast. The flowers are 1½ inches wide and white to light or medium pink with a darker throat. Blooms are fragrant and appear early. It is a medium to large shrub. Hardy to –10° F.

R. flammeum
(syn. R. speciosum)

This species is native to Georgia and South Carolina. The flowers range from yellowish orange to reddish orange, and are marked with a large orange blotch. A low to tall heat-tolerant shrub that blooms early midseason. Hardy to –10° F.

R. occidentale
(Pacific azalea)

This native of the Pacific Coast has 2½-inch-wide flowers that are very fragrant. They have a yellow blotch and vary from white to pink and reddish. It is very difficult to grow in the East.

R. periclymenoides
(syn. R. nudiflorum)
(Pinxterbloom azalea)

The fragrant, white to pinkish flowers, 1½ inches wide, bloom midseason. A native to the East, this medium shrub spreads by stolons. Hardy to –15° F.

R. prinophyllum
(syn. R. roseum)
(Roseshell azalea)

This very hardy plant is native to the Northeast. The fragrant flowers are pale to deep pink, 1½ inches wide, and bloom midseason. Hardy to –30° F.

R. prunifolium
(Plum-leaved azalea)

Native to Georgia, this plant is valued for its late blooms (in July and August). The flowers are reddish orange and 1½ inches wide. Hardy to –5° F.

Rhododendron yedoense *var.* poukhanense

Adolphe Audusson

R. schlippenbachii
(Royal azalea)

The royal azalea is a tall shrub native to Korea. The early-blooming, fragrant flowers are light purplish pink to vivid pink. Blossoms are 2 to 4 inches wide. The leaves are 3 to 5 inches long, in whorls of five. This is a beautiful shrub when growing well, but it is fussy. For best performance, maintain a soil pH of 6.5 and supplement the soil with calcium. A white form with a reddish brown dotted throat is available. Hardy to –10° F.

R. vaseyi
(Pinkshell azalea)

This species is native to only four mountain counties in North Carolina at elevations above 3,500 feet. The fragrant, pink flowers are 1½ inches wide, and the petals are deeply divided. The shrub is medium to large. 'White Find' is a good white selection. Hardy to –20° F.

R. viscosum
(Swamp azalea)

This species is native to eastern North America. The base of the fragrant, white flower is a long slender tube 1 to 1½ inches long, which terminates in short lobes, 1 to 1¼ inches wide. The plant blooms midseason and spreads by stolons. Hardy to –20° F.

R. yedoense var.
poukhanense
(Korean azalea)

A medium, early-blooming shrub native to Korea, which is often mistakenly listed as the species *R. poukhanense*. The single flowers are mildly fragrant and 1½ to 2 inches wide. They are light to medium purple with a reddish blotch. Each blossom has 10 stamens. The plant is semideciduous, losing most of its leaves in colder

climates. The Korean azalea has played an important role in the development of hardier evergreen azaleas in Europe and the United States. Hardy to about –15° F.

R. yedoense
(Yodogawa azalea)

This double-flowered garden form, found before the single-flowered variety *R. yedoense* var. *poukhanense*, was described as a species. The fragrant, 2-inch-wide, double flowers are light purple, blooming early. It is a medium shrub that is semievergreen to deciduous in colder climates. Hardy to about –15° F.

CAMELLIAS

This section is divided into six major groups: *Camellia japonica, Camellia reticulata, Camellia sasanqua,* Higo camellias, other camellia hybrids, and camellia species.

The Camellia Society has developed six classifications for camellia flower forms: single, semidouble, anemone, peony, rose form double, and formal double. See page 13 for examples of these forms.

The flower sizes are described as follows.
Miniature: up to 2½ inches wide
Small: 2½ to 3 inches wide
Medium: 3 to 4 inches wide
Large: 4 to 5 inches wide
Very large: more than 5 inches wide

The blooming seasons are classified as early (early fall through December); midseason (January through mid-March); and late (late March and later). Of course, these flowering periods are variable. Unusually warm or cold weather conditions can affect a particular variety's bloom season by several weeks. Also, camellias planted in colder climates will bloom later than those grown in warmer regions.

Betty Sheffield Supreme

Are-Jishi

Camellia japonica

The cultivars of *Camellia japonica* are the best known of the camellias. Japonicas can endure occasional drops in temperature to near 0° F but will not survive long periods of freezing, windy weather. A few varieties are more cold hardy and can tolerate temperatures as low as –5° F for short periods of time. Because flowers and flower buds are not as cold hardy as the plants, midseason-flowering varieties are likely to lose their flower buds during the winter months. Therefore, early- and late-blooming varieties are best for colder areas of the South. In even colder climates, where winter temperatures drop low enough to kill the plants, camellias can be grown in a lathhouse or cool greenhouse, where they make excellent tub specimens. The camellias described in this section include many old favorites and award-winning plants. The awards were all given by the American Camellia Society.

Adolphe Audusson (syn. 'Adolphe', 'Audrey Hopfer')

This is an award-winning, reliable old French variety. The large, dark red flowers are semidouble and bloom midseason. It is a medium-sized plant with a compact growth habit. Two sports are 'Adolphe Audusson Special', which has predominately white flowers, and a variegated form with dark red flowers spotted with white.

Alba Plena

One of the oldest camellias in cultivation, this variety is mentioned in an early Chinese manuscript. The flowers are white, medium, and formal double, and the slow-growing plant has a bushy growth habit. An award-winning and popular variety.

Alison Leigh Woodroof

The small, semidouble flowers appear midseason and are pale pink turning to vivid pink at the edge. The plant has a vigorous, upright growth habit.

Angel's Blush

This is a midseason, miniature variety with pink semidouble flowers.

Are-Jishi (syn. 'Aloha', 'Beni-Are-Jishi', 'Callie')

This old variety was imported from Japan. It is an early-flowering variety especially appropriate for colder areas. The full peony form flowers are strong to medium red, and the plant is vigorous with an open, upright growth habit. A variegated form is available.

Ave Maria

This popular modern camellia has small to medium, silvery pink, formal flowers that bloom early to midseason. The plant grows slowly and has a compact habit.

Berenice Boddy

This is a cold-hardy variety. The medium, semidouble flowers are light pink, with the backs of the petals a darker pink. The plant grows vigorously, has an upright habit, and blooms midseason to late.

Betty Sheffield

This popular and award-winning camellia has medium to large, semidouble to loose peony form flowers that are white with red to pink stripes and blotches. It is a medium to large plant with a compact growth habit, blooming midseason. It sports freely and has produced several well-known varieties.

Betty Sheffield Supreme

The large, loose, informal double flowers have a deep pink to rose-red border on each petal. The width of the colorful margin varies with each flower. This beautiful camellia blooms midseason and is a must for mild climates. It is an excellent cool greenhouse plant.

Black Tie

The small, dark red formal double flowers resemble a rosebud. A vigorous, upright plant that blooms midseason to late.

Debutante

Dr. Tinsley

Carter's Sunburst

Flame

Blood of China
(syn. 'Victor Emmanuel', 'Alice Slack')
The deep reddish orange, slightly fragrant medium flowers are semidouble to loose peony form, and open late. This old standard variety is still popular.

Bob Hope
The large, semidouble flowers of this striking camellia are an intense dark red with purple-black markings on the buds and petals, blooming in midseason.

Carter's Sunburst
The large to very large, pastel pink flower has darker pink stripes and mottling. The flower form is semidouble to peony to formal double. The blooms of this award-winning plant are borne throughout the season, from early to late.

China Doll
The medium to large, white flower is blushed pale pink and edged with yellow-pink margins. The flower has a loose, high-centered peony form. It is a compact plant.

Christmas Beauty
The large, early-blooming, vivid red flowers are semidouble with fluted petals. The plant is vigorous and upright with pendulous branches.

C. M. Wilson
(syn. 'Gracie Burhard', 'Lucille Ferrell')
This is a sport of 'Elegans'. The large to very large, light pink flowers bloom from early to midseason.

Daikagura
This great old standard variety was developed in Japan. The medium to large, peony form flowers are deep pink splotched with white. The slow-growing plant has a compact growth habit and blooms early. The flowers are extremely variable.

Debutante
This is an award-winning plant with full peony form flowers. The attractive, medium blooms are pastel pink and bloom on a vigorous, upright plant early to midseason.

Dr. Tinsley
The beautiful, semidouble flowers are very pale pink that turn to deeper pink. The yellow stamens contrast nicely and give the flowers a roselike appearance. The plant blooms midseason and has a compact, upright habit. It is a cold-hardy variety.

Donckelarii
The large, semidouble, midseason flowers of this old standard variety are red marbled with white. This award winner has produced many named sports, such as the popular 'Ville de Nantes'.

Drama Girl
This award-winning plant has very large, semidouble flowers of a deep yellow-pink. Flowers bloom midseason on pendulous branches. The plant has a vigorous, open habit; in order to maintain a compact plant, annual pruning is required.

Eleanor Hagood
The pale pink, medium flowers are formal double. The plant is especially good for cooler climates because it blooms late.

Elegans
(syn. 'Chandleri Elegans')
This well-known camellia has large, anemone form, deep pink flowers. The central petal-like stamens are pink spotted with white. This slow-spreading plant blooms early to midseason. The award-winning plant has produced many sports.

Elegans Champagne
This beautiful sport of 'Elegans Splendor' blooms early to midseason. The large, anemone flower is white with a creamy white petaloid center (have petal-like stamens). The leaf margins are finely toothed. The plant is bushy and spreading.

Elegans Splendor
The early to midseason flowers of this award-winning plant are light pink edged with white. The margins of the petals and leaves are deeply toothed.

Guilio Nuccio

Herme

Elegans Supreme

This popular sport of 'Elegans' has rose-pink flowers and petals with deeply toothed margins. It is a compact plant with wavy leaves and blooms early to mid-season.

Fircone Variegated

This award-winning plant has miniature, semidouble flowers of deep red mottled with white. It is a sport of 'Fircone', which has red flowers.

Flame

The large, semidouble flowers are deep reddish orange with prominent yellow stamens. This vigorous, upright plant blooms late and is a good cold-hardy variety.

Flowerwood

This is a fimbriated (the flowers have fringed petals) sport of 'Mathotiana'. The large, formal to formal double flowers are vivid red with a slight purplish cast. The plant is vigorous with a compact habit, blooming midseason to late.

Glen 40

The large, deep red flowers of this very popular variety are formal to rose form double. It is a slow-growing plant with a compact, upright habit, blooming midseason to late. A variegated form, 'Glen 40 Var', is available.

Governor Mouton
(syn. 'Aunt Jetty', 'Angelica')

This old variety has a medium, reddish orange flower splotched with white. The form is semidouble to loose peony. Vigorous and upright, the plant blooms midseason to late.

Grace Albritton

This popular, award-winning camellia has small, formal double flowers that are light pink edged in deeper pink.

Grand Slam

This is a popular award winner with a very large, vivid red flower. The bloom is semidouble to anemone. A vigorous grower, the plant has an upright habit and blooms midseason.

Guilio Nuccio

The very large flower is a deep yellow-pink semidouble with irregular, wavy petals. This vigorous, upright award winner blooms midseason.

Helen Bower

The award-winning large flowers are a strong red with a purplish tint and occasional white markings. The blooms are rose form double and appear midseason to late.

Herme
(syn. 'Jordan's Pride')

This is a beautiful old variety from Japan, where it is called 'Hikaru Genji'. The semidouble, pink flower is streaked with deeper pink and has an irregular white border. It is a midseason bloomer.

High Hat

This light pink sport of 'Daikagura' has large, peony form flowers and blooms early. It has produced a white sport, 'Conrad Hilton'.

Kewpie Doll

The flower is a neat, light pink, miniature anemone form with a petaloid center. It blooms midseason.

King's Ransom

The pastel pink flower deepens to deep pink as it matures. The form is loose with a petaloid center. The plant blooms midseason.

Kramer's Supreme

The large, vivid red, slightly fragrant flower with a tint of orange is peony form. The plant is vigorous with dense, upright growth and blooms midseason.

K. Sawada

This variety has beautiful, white, formal to rose form double flowers. The plant is vigorous, has a semi-upright habit, and blooms midseason.

Kumasaka

This is a very old variety from Japan. The flower is medium, rose-pink, and varies from a rose form double to peony form.

Man Size

Nuccio's Pearl

Lady Clare
(syn. 'Empress')

An award-winning, old variety from Japan, this has the Japanese name 'Akashigata'. The large, deep pink flowers have prominent yellow stamens and bloom early to midseason. A variegated sport, 'Oniji', is also available.

Lady Kay

This beautiful sport of 'Ville de Nantes' is similar in form. The large, red flowers are blotched white, and the form is loose to full peony. Petals are occasionally fimbriated (fringed). A popular, award-winning variety, it has a red sport, 'Lady Kay Red'.

Lady Vansittart

This is an old but popular variety. The flowers are medium, semidouble, and have broad wavy petals. The color is extremely variable but usually white with a faint blush and stripes of light pink. It is a slow-growing, bushy plant with deeply toothed leaves. It is cold hardy.

Little Slam

This award-winning red miniature has full peony form flowers and blooms early to midseason.

Magnoliaeflora

This is an old, but still popular, award-winning variety. The very pale pink flowers are semidouble with prominent yellow stamens.

Man Size

This outstanding white miniature is the recipient of many awards. The white, anemone form flowers bloom midseason.

Margaret Davis

The white to pale yellow-white flowers are full peony form. The petals are edged in a vivid red. A midseason bloomer, this is the winner of many awards.

Mathotiana

This popular old variety has large to very large flowers of crimson in rose form to formal double. The award-winning plant blooms midseason to late.

Mathotiana Supreme

This beautiful sport of 'Mathotiana' has semidouble, crimson flowers that are very large with loose, irregular petals and yellow stamens. Occasionally, the flowers are blotched with white.

Miss Charleston

The large, deep red flowers of this award-winning camellia are semidouble with a high center. The plant blooms midseason. A variegated form is available.

Mrs. D. W. Davis

This camellia has beautiful, very large, pale pink, semidouble flowers with prominent yellow stamens. Occasionally, the flowers are petaloid (have petal-like stamens). This prize-winning plant is dense and vigorous, and it blooms midseason.

Mrs. Tingley

The formal double, yellow-pink flower blooms midseason to late. The plant is compact and fairly cold hardy.

Nuccio's Gem

The beautiful flower of this very popular camellia is white and formal double. The award-winning plant is vigorous with dense, glossy growth, and blooms early to midseason.

Nuccio's Pearl

The beautifully formed, double, pale pink flower is edged with a deeper shade of pink. The flowers bloom midseason on a compact plant that is an excellent container specimen.

Pink Pagoda

The large, deep pink, formal double flower has wavy petals. The plant blooms early to midseason. 'Pink Frost' is a pink sport with faint white margins on the petals.

Pink Perfection

This very popular, award-winning camellia is known worldwide. The shell pink, small, formal double flower has a long flowering period, from early to late.

Tiffany

Tomorrow's Dawn

Prelude
The flower is vivid red, with a semidouble to anemone form. The growth is vigorous and dense, and the plant blooms early to midseason. A variegated sport is available.

Professor Charles S. Sargent
This is a cold-hardy variety, blooming midseason. The dark red flowers have an anemone center but are also described as having a loose peony form. The plant is frequently nicknamed 'Christmas Carnation' in the South. A variegated sport is available.

R. L. Wheeler
This beautiful, popular, award-winning variety has deep pink, very large flowers with a semidouble to anemone form and a solid circle of stamens. The plant is vigorous and upright, and blooms early to midseason. A variegated sport is available.

Sawada's Dream
The perfect formal double flower is white in the center with the outer third shaded a pale pink. The petals are pointed and well formed. This recipient of the National Hall of Fame Award blooms midseason.

Sea Foam
This camellia has large, white, formal double flowers. The plant is late blooming, with an upright growth habit.

**September Morn
(syn. 'Yohei Haku')**
This very early variety is good for cooler areas. The white to pale pink flowers are semidouble to peony to anemone.

Silver Chalice
This is one of the best whites. The large flowers are a full peony form and bloom midseason. The fluted, upright petals give a rounded effect.

Snow Baby
This camellia has white, miniature flowers in midseason. The flower is an anemone form.

Snowman
The large, white, semidouble flower blooms midseason. This award-winning plant has a spreading, upright growth habit.

Spring Sonnet
The semidouble flowers are pale pink with darker pink margins. The plant blooms midseason.

Swan Lake
This is a beautiful rose form double with white, ruffled petals. The plant is vigorous and compact, and blooms midseason.

Thelma Dale
This midseason to late bloomer is good for cooler climates. The light purplish pink flowers are semidouble to rose form double.

Tiffany
The flower form of this beautiful award winner varies from loose to peony to anemone. Flowers are large to very large, and are a light purple-pink that turns to a deeper pink at the margins. The plant is vigorous and has an upright habit.

Tomorrow
This camellia is a real prize, with large to very large, vivid red flowers. The blooms are semidouble, with irregular petals and large petal-like stamens, to full peony form. The plant blooms early to midseason. This vigorous plant has an open growth habit and slightly pendulous branches, and has produced many sports.

Tomorrow Park Hill
The large flowers of this award-winning camellia are pale pink, shading toward a deeper pink at the petal margins. There are occasional white variations.

Tomorrow's Dawn
This beautiful sport of 'Tomorrow' has won several awards. The flowers are pale pink, lightening toward white edges. The flowers occasionally have white petal-like stamens and red streaks.

Ville de Nantes

Captain Rawes

Ville de Nantes

This is an old, but still popular, award-winning variety with medium to large, semidouble, fringed flowers. The upright petals are dark red with white blotches, and the blooms appear midseason to late.

Vulcan

The large to very large, vivid red flowers are semidouble to formal double. The center petals are often irregular, faintly streaked, and have blotches of white. The plant is vigorous, with an upright growth habit, and it blooms early to midseason. A variegated sport is available.

Woodville Red

This old variety has large, deep vivid red, peony form flowers. The plant blooms midseason.

Camellia reticulata

The third most popular camellia is *C. reticulata*, a small to medium-sized tree native to southern China.

The reticulatas are not as cold hardy as other camellia species. Their lower limit is 25° F. However, they have not been thoroughly tested, and variation in hardiness is to be expected. Most of the reticulatas growing in the western United States are thought to be hybrids of *C. reticulata* with other species. Over three hundred reticulatas are registered. The following list contains *C. reticulata* and hybrids with reticulata parentage.

Buddha

One of the early reticulata hybrids, this camellia was introduced from China. The very large, deep pink flowers are semidouble with irregular, upright, wavy petals. The flowers bloom midseason to late.

Captain Rawes

The very large, deep pink flowers are semidouble to loose peony in form. The plant is vigorous and upright, and blooms late.

China Lady

The very large, strong purple-pink flowers are semidouble with irregularly shaped petals.

Crimson Robe
(syn. 'Dataohong')

This is an award-winning, popular cultivar. The semidouble, red flowers are very large, and the petals are wavy and crinkled. The plant has a vigorous, spreading growth habit, and the leaves are sometimes variegated with a yellowish white margin.

Dr. Clifford Parks

The very large, reddish orange flower is loose to full peony to anemone in form. It is a spectacular flower and has received several awards.

Francie L

A recipient of several awards, this variety has very large, deep pink, semidouble flowers with irregular, wavy petals. It is one of the most cold hardy of the reticulata hybrids.

Jean Pursel

The peony form flower is very large and light purple-pink. Pale pink to white petal-like stamens emerge from the center of the flower. Blooms appear midseason to late. The award-winning plant is vigorous, with an upright growth habit.

Lasca Beauty

The semidouble, pale pink flower of this award winner is very large. This open, upright plant blooms midseason.

Nuccio's Ruby

This gem has large to very large, vivid dark red flowers. The blooms are semidouble with irregular, ruffled petals. The habit is upright and bushy, and the plant blooms midseason. A variegated form is available.

Pagoda

This reticulata from China is often called by its Chinese name, 'Songzlin'. The flower is large, formal double to rose form double, and a deep reddish orange. It's a midseason bloomer.

Lasca Beauty

Bonanza

Jean May

Purple Gown
(syn. 'Zipao', 'Tzipao')

The large to very large flower is formal double to peony in form and has wavy petals of deep purplish red with white markings. The compact plant blooms profusely in midseason.

Shot Silk
(syn. 'Dayiuhong')

This beautiful introduction from China has very large, semidouble flowers of a striking vivid pink. The petals have wavy margins. This is an early-blooming camellia.

Valentine Day

This recipient of several awards is considered one of the perfect reticulata hybrids. The very large, formal double flower of a deep pink to reddish orange has a rosebud center.

Camellia sasanqua

The camellias collectively known as sasanquas include varieties and hybrids of three species: *C. sasanqua, C. hiemalis,* and *C. vernalis.* The species *C. sasanqua* is native to Japan. The two other species, *C. hiemalis* and *C. vernalis*, were never found in the wild and are known only as garden specimens. Botanically, they should be listed as hybrids of *C. sasanqua* and possibly *C. japonica.* Both flower later than typical sasanquas.

The sasanquas bloom in the fall and are more tender than the japonicas. Good as landscape plants, the sasanquas make excellent foundation, hedge, and screen plantings. Some plants are also used as ground covers, espaliers, and container specimens.

Bettie Patricia

This is a popular, light pink, rose form double sasanqua. The plant is upright and spreading.

Bonanza

This award-winning sasanqua has large, deep red, semidouble flowers that bloom in early fall. The petals are wavy and fluted.

Bonsai Baby

The small, deep red flowers are formal double to rose form double. The plant is a compact cultivar of *C. hiemalis* and a favorite container and bonsai plant.

Chansonette

This award-winning *C. hiemalis* cultivar has large, pink flowers. The semidouble blooms have ruffled petals. It is a bushy plant and flowers in late fall.

Cleopatra

This sasanqua has light to deep pink, semidouble flowers and a bushy growth habit. Two sports are available: 'Cleopatra Blush', with pale pink flowers, and 'Cleopatra White', with white flowers.

Cotton Candy

This popular sasanqua has an upright, spreading habit and large, pink, semidouble flowers with ruffled petals.

Dawn
(syn. 'Ginryu', 'Ginryo')

This cultivar of *C. vernalis* has semidouble flowers that are white blushed with pink. It blooms in late fall, and the blossoms last a long time on the plant, so it is susceptible to damage by an early freeze.

Dazzler

The deep pink to red flowers of this *C. hiemalis* cultivar are semidouble with wavy petals. 'Dazzler' is a vigorous plant with a spreading, upright habit.

Jean May

This popular landscape plant and container specimen has large, pink, double flowers that provide a beautiful fall display. It is best used in partial shade because the flowers often fade in direct sun.

Yuletide

Narumigata

Shishi Gashira

Kelly McKnight
This popular variety is noted for its brilliant red, long-lasting, small rose form double flowers.

Mine No Yuki
(syn. 'Snow', 'Snow on the Mountain', 'White Dove')
A very popular sasanqua, this bushy plant produces an abundance of semidouble white flowers that literally cover the plant in late fall. It is an excellent landscape plant as well as a container specimen.

Narumigata
This vigorous, upright sasanqua has large, white, single flowers shaded light pink. The blooms are cup-shaped and have a crinkled texture. This cultivar is often called 'Oleifera', but it should not be confused with *C. oleifera*.

Our Linda
This sasanqua has excellent, pink, rose form double flowers. It has an upright and dense habit.

Pink Snow
The large, light pink, semidouble flowers are often faintly blushed with purple. The plant is bushy and blooms late.

Setsugekka
(syn. 'Elegant Friend', 'Fluted White', 'Wavy White')
This favorite sasanqua has large, white, semidouble flowers with ruffled petals. The plant has a vigorous, upright habit and displays the flowers very well.

Shishi Gashira
(syn. 'Lion Head')
This popular, late-blooming *C. hiemalis* cultivar has deep pink flowers, semidouble to double, with fluted petals. The plant has a compact habit.

Showa No Sakae
(syn. 'Glory', 'Usubeni')
This *C. hiemalis* cultivar has semidouble to rose form double, light pink flowers. Sometimes the flowers are marbled with white. This is a low-growing, compact camellia good as a landscaping plant, an espalier, and a container specimen. It blooms early.

Sparkling Burgundy
This very popular sasanqua is noted for its excellent floral display. The small, peony form flowers are deep purple-pink with a light purple blush. It is a tall, upright, spreading plant.

Star Above Star
This is an award-winning, late-flowering cultivar of *C. vernalis*. The semidouble flowers are white, changing to purplish pink at the edges. The petals are crinkled, and the flower has a starlike appearance.

Tanya
This popular sasanqua was named for the title of a Japanese drama. The small, single flowers are deep pink with prominent yellow stamens. The plant is low, with small leaves and a bushy, spreading habit. It makes a good ground cover.

Wave Crest
This very attractive sasanqua has large, white flowers with long, narrow petals that are wavy and ragged, giving the blossoms a distinctive look.

Yuletide
An award-winning favorite, this sasanqua bears its small, single, reddish orange flowers in profusion. The petals are broad and rounded, setting off the mass of yellow stamens nicely. 'Yuletide' is a compact plant, excellent for the landscape and as a container specimen. It blooms late.

Higo Camellias
The Higo camellias are an old group of japonica cultivars that were unknown to the Western world until the early nineteenth century. These hybrid plants were mainly from the Japanese island of Kyushu and were not exported. Higo was the name of the district in which these plants were developed. The Higo camellias are hybrids of selected cultivars of *C. japonica* with *C. japonica rusticana*, a cold-hardy subspecies of *C. japonica*. The unique Higo

Tenju

Angel Wings

flowers are nearly all singles with flat petals. Each flower has a multitude of stamens (one hundred to two hundred). The stamens are arranged in a decorative, tight hemisphere in the center of the flower. The blooms vary from solid shades of white, pink, and red to patterns of blotches and stripes. Some of the flowers are fragrant. In Japan, Higo camellias are generally used as bonsai or container plants. They are mainly used as landscape plants in the United States. Over twenty cultivars are currently available in the United States.

Asagao
The medium, single flower is pale pink with flared stamens. The plant blooms early to midseason and has a bushy habit.

Hi-No-Maru
The single, medium flower is red, and the petals are wavy. Blooms appear midseason. Growth is slow, upright, and compact.

Jitsu-Getsu-Sei
The single, medium flowers are red splotched with white. Blooms are flat with flared stamens. The plant is vigorous with an upright growth habit, and blooms appear midseason to late.

Mangetsu
The single, medium, white flower has golden, flared stamens. It is a vigorous, upright grower and blooms midseason.

Shin-Tsukasa-Nishiki
The medium, single flower is deep pink with rose-pink stripes. Stamens are flared, and some of them are petal-like. The petals are wavy. The plant has a bushy, upright growth habit and blooms midseason.

Tenju
The medium to large, single, blush-pink flower has flared stamens. The plant is a vigorous grower, with an open, upright habit. The flowers appear midseason.

Other Camellia Hybrids
After the introduction of *Camellia japonica* and its many cultivars, interest in the other camellia species slowly developed in England. In 1942, J. C. Williams made the first cross between the two species *C. saluenensis* and *C. japonica*. Subsequent hybrids of these two species are now known as the Williamsii hybrids. Later, hybridizers began to cross other species and cultivars with newly discovered species. The hardiness of many of these hybrids is not known and is assumed to be similar to that of *C. japonica*. With further testing, some may prove to be more hardy than others. Over three hundred camellia hybrids are registered. The following list includes hybrid camellias with parents other than *C. reticulata*.

Ack-Scent
The delightfully fragrant, peony form flower is light pink. The plant blooms midseason to late.

Angel Wings
The semidouble flowers are white shaded with purplish pink, and the narrow, wavy petals are upright. Blooms appear midseason.

Anticipation
This award-winning Williamsii hybrid has large, deep pink, peony form flowers. They bloom midseason. A variegated sport is available.

Baby Bear
The small, single flowers of this attractive, miniature camellia are light pink with occasional white blotches. The dwarf plant blooms midseason.

Charlean
The beautiful, large, semidouble pink flower with faint purplish overtones has pink stamens tipped with yellow. The award-winning plant is vigorous with a spreading habit, and blooms midseason to late.

Fragrant Pink Improved

Camellia chrysantha

Cornish Snow
The small, single flowers are white, sometimes blushed with pink. The plant blooms heavily midseason to late. It has an open growth habit with pendulous branches.

Donation
The large, light purple-pink flowers of this award-winning Williamsii are semidouble, blooming midseason. It is a vigorous plant with dense, upright growth. A variegated sport is available.

Fragrant Pink
This lightly scented, miniature camellia has small, deep pink, peony form flowers. They bloom early to late. 'Fragrant Pink Improved' is a form with larger flowers.

Garden Glory
The light purple-pink, rose form double flower of this Williamsii hybrid has notched petals. It is a good espalier plant and blooms early to late.

Pink Bouquet
The light pink, medium to large flower is semidouble. The plant blooms heavily midseason.

Camellia Species
The genus *Camellia* consists of over two hundred species. Most are not available in the western world. Many are less hardy than *C. japonica* and *C. sasanqua*. The following are some of the more common and readily available species.

C. chrysantha
This rare, yellow species from China was introduced to the western world in 1980 and bloomed for the first time during the 1984–1985 season. The small, single to semidouble, yellow flower has shiny, heavily textured petals. The plant is vigorous with an upright, open habit and blooms midseason. This species will be limited in availability for many years.

C. crapnelliana
The small flower is white. The bark of this species is reddish brown.

C. cuspidata
Native to southern China, this species has small, single, white flowers. It blooms midseason. The leaves are pointed.

C. fraterna
The mildly fragrant, small, single flower of this native of central China is white flushed with pale purple. The flowers are in small clusters and bloom midseason. The small shrub has elliptic leaves.

C. granthamiana
The large, white flower has clusters of prominent yellow stamens. Leaves are large, to 4 inches long, with wrinkled surfaces. The only known existing wild plant is a small tree in Hong Kong.

C. hiemalis
The bloom closely resembles that of the sasanquas, but it appears later. It is known only as a garden form and has produced many varieties.

C. hongkongensis
The large flowers are crimson with somewhat velvety petals on the back. The leathery leaves are dark green on top and light green on the underside.

C. japonica
This small tree—native to Japan, Korea, and eastern China—has deep pink to red flowers in the wild. It is best known in its numerous garden forms.

Camellia hongkongensis

Camellia yuhsienensis

C. lutchuensis
The small, white flower is very fragrant. The leaves are small and sharply pointed. Blooms appear midseason. This species is much used in hybridizing for fragrance.

C. maliflora
(syn. 'Betty McCaskill')
Native to central China, this species has small, pink, semi-double flowers. Leaves are small and pointed. The plant blooms midseason to late.

C. oleifera
This species has fragrant, single, white flowers. Its growth habit is upright to semi-cascading. A native of China, it is cultivated there for its seed oil. It blooms midseason.

C. reticulata
Many garden varieties and hybrids are available of this native of southern China.

C. rosiflora
The small, single flower is pink. This species is a large shrub or small tree and blooms in midseason.

C. salicifolia
The small, single flower is white and slightly fragrant. Leaves are long and narrow, and the growth habit is low and bushy. This plant, a native of Hong Kong and Formosa, blooms midseason.

C. saluenensis
The small, single flower of this native of southern China is white flushed light to deep pink. Blooms appear midseason to late.

C. sasanqua
This native of southern Japan and the Ryukyu Islands has white to pink flowers. It is a large shrub or small tree.

C. sinensis
This is the commercial tea plant of Asia. It is a large shrub or small tree with small, white, single flowers. The medium, upright plants bloom midseason and are generally hardier than C. japonica.

C. transnokensis
The slow-growing shrub has very small, single, white flowers. The leaves are small and narrow, and the growth habit is narrow and upright.

C. tsaii
This shrub or small tree of southern China has small, single, white flowers. The slender leaves are waxy. Flowers bloom midseason.

C. vernalis
The origin of this species is unknown; it is found only as a garden plant. It is very similar to C. sasanqua but blooms later.

C. yuhsienensis
The very small, fragrant, single, white flowers bloom in great profusion in midseason.

Some Resources

RHODODENDRON AND AZALEA SOCIETIES

If you become interested in camellias, rhododendrons, or azaleas, consider joining a plant society. These organizations publish informative periodicals and hold national and regional meetings. As a member, you will have the chance to share ideas with people of similar interests. Here are the addresses to write for information.

American Camellia Society One Massee Lane, Fort Valley, GA 31030 (912) 967-2358

American Rhododendron Society Box 1380, Gloucester, VA 23061 (804) 693-4433

The Azalea Society of America Box 34536, West Bethesda, MD 20827-0536

Rhododendron Society of Canada 5200 Timothy Crescent, Niagara Falls, Ont. L2E 5G3

Rhododendron Species Foundation Box 3798, Federal Way, WA 98063 (206) 661-9377

FAMOUS CAMELLIA, RHODODENDRON, AND AZALEA GARDENS

Bellingrath Gardens Theodore, AL. *Camellias*

Biltmore House Asheville, NC. *Azaleas*

Brookside Gardens Wheaton, MD. *Azaleas and rhododendrons*

Butchart Gardens Victoria, B.C., Canada. *Rhododendrons*

Callaway Gardens Pine Mountain, GA. *Azaleas*

Crystal Springs Rhododendron Garden Portland, OR. *Azaleas, rhododendrons*

Cypress Gardens Charleston, SC. *Azaleas, camellias*

Descanso Gardens La Cañada, CA. *Camellias*

Florida Cypress Gardens Winterhaven, FL. *Azaleas, camellias*

Hendricks Park and Rhododendron Garden Eugene, OR. *Azaleas, rhododendrons*

Heritage Plantation Sandwich, MA. *Rhododendrons*

Hodges Gardens Many, LA. *Azaleas, camellias*

Holden Arboretum Cleveland, OH. *Azaleas, rhododendrons*

Huntington Botanical Garden San Marino, CA. *Camellias*

Longwood Gardens Kennett Square, PA. *Camellias*

Maclay Gardens Tallahassee, FL. *Azaleas, camellias*

Magnolia Plantation and Gardens Charleston, SC. *Azaleas, camellias*

Massee Lane Gardens American Camellia Society, Fort Valley, GA. *Camellias*

Meerkerk Rhododendron Garden Whidbey Island, WA. *Rhododendrons*

Mendocino Botanical Gardens Mendocino, CA. *Azaleas, rhododendrons*

Middleton Place Charleston, SC. *Azaleas, camellias*

Missouri Botanical Gardens St. Louis, MO. *Camellias*

Norfolk Botanical Gardens Norfolk, VA. *Azaleas, rhododendrons, camellias*

Orton Plantation Wilmington, NC. *Azaleas, camellias*

Planting Fields Arboretum Oyster Bay, NY. *Azaleas, rhododendrons, camellias*

Rhododendron Species Botanical Garden Federal Way, WA. *Azalea and rhododendron species*

Scott Arboretum of Swarthmore College (including Wister Garden) Swarthmore, PA. *Azaleas, camellias*

Strybing Arboretum San Francisco, CA. *Rhododendrons*

United States National Arboretum Washington, DC. *Azaleas, camellias*

University of California Botanical Garden Berkeley, CA. *Rhododendrons*

Winterthur Wilmington, DE. *Azaleas, rhododendrons*

SOURCES OF PLANTS

It is always better to purchase plants from a local nursery, where you can see items before buying them, and where you don't have to pay shipping costs. But if you can't find the plants you want locally, here are some mail-order sources. Only azalea, rhododendron, and camellia specialists are included here; many general nurseries also carry these plants.

Azalea Hill Gardens and Nursery 1006 South Evans Road, Pine Bluff, AR 71602 (501) 247-1574. *Hardy and newer varieties of azaleas*

The Bovees Nursery 1737 Southwest Coronado Street, Portland, OR 97219 (503) 244-9341. *Unusual rhododendrons, especially Vireya rhododendrons*

Camellia Forest Nursery 125 Carolina Forest Road, Chapel Hill, NC 27516 (919) 967-5529. *Camellias, specializing in hardy varieties*

Carlson's Gardens Box 305, South Salem, NY 10590 (914) 763-5958. *Large selection of hardy azaleas and rhododendrons*

V. O. Chambers Nursery 26874 Ferguson Road, Junction City, OR 97448 (503) 998-2467. *A wide variety of azaleas and rhododendrons*

The Cummins Garden 22 Robertsville Road, Marlboro, NJ 07746 (908) 536-2591. *Dwarf rhododendrons*

Eastern Plant Specialties Box 226, Georgetown, ME 04548 (800) Will-Grow, (207) 371-2888. *Hardy azaleas and rhododendrons*

Five Star Gardens 9625 Northwest Roy Road, Forest Grove, OR 97116 Fax: (503) 357-6792. *Rhododendrons and azaleas, some camellias*

The Greenery 14450 Northeast 16th Place, Bellevue, WA 98007 (206) 641-1458 Fax: (206) 643-3844. *Azalea and rhododendron species, dwarf and small-growing hybrids*

Greer Gardens 1280 Goodpasture Island Road, Eugene, OR 97401 (800) 548-0111, (503) 686-8266 Fax: (503) 686-0910. *Rhododendrons and azaleas*

James Harris Nursery 538 Swanson Drive, Lawrenceville, GA 30243 (404) 963-7463. *Harris hybrid azaleas*

Hillhouse Nursery 90 Kresson–Gibbsboro Road, Voorhees, NJ 08043 (609) 784-6203. *Linwood azaleas*

Holly Hills, Inc. 1216 Hillsdale Road, Evansville, IN 47711 (812) 867-3367. *Schroeder hybrid azaleas*

Kelleygreen Rhododendron Nursery 6924 Highway 38, Drain, OR 97435 (503) 836-2290. *Rhododendrons and azaleas*

Mowbray Gardens 3318 Mowbray Lane, Cincinnati, OH 45226 (513) 321-0694. *Rare and hardy rhododendrons*

Nuccio's Nursery Box 6160, Altadena, CA 91003 (818) 794-3383. *Wide variety of camellias and azaleas*

Southern Plants Box 232, Semmes, AL 36575 (205) 649-5221. *Azaleas*

Stubbs Shrubs 37235 SE Lusted Road, Sandy, OR 97009 (503) 638-5048 Fax: (503) 659-4466. *Evergreen azaleas*

Westgate Gardens Nursery 751 Westgate Drive, Eureka, CA 95503 (707) 442-1239. *Azaleas and rhododendrons*

Whitney Gardens Nursery Box F, 31600 Highway 101, Brinnon, WA 98320-0080 (800) 952-2404. *Azaleas and rhododendrons*

Bob Wines Nursery 2610 Southeast 38th Street, Ocala, FL 34471 (904) 629-5766. *Camellias*

U.S. Measure and Metric Measure Conversion Chart

Formulas for Exact Measures

	Symbol	When you know:	Multiply by:	To find:
Mass (weight)	oz	ounces	28.35	grams
	lb	pounds	0.45	kilograms
	g	grams	0.035	ounces
	kg	kilograms	2.2	pounds
Volume	pt	pints	0.47	liters
	qt	quarts	0.95	liters
	gal	gallons	3.785	liters
	ml	milliliters	0.034	fluid ounces
Length	in.	inches	2.54	centimeters
	ft	feet	30.48	centimeters
	yd	yards	0.9144	meters
	mi	miles	1.609	kilometers
	km	kilometers	0.621	miles
	m	meters	1.094	yards
	cm	centimeters	0.39	inches
Temperature	°F	Fahrenheit	$\frac{5}{9}$ (after subtracting 32)	Celsius
	°C	Celsius	$\frac{9}{5}$ (then add 32)	Fahrenheit
Area	in.^{2}	square inches	6.452	square centimeters
	ft^2	square feet	929.0	square centimeters
	yd^2	square yards	8361.0	square centimeters
	a.	acres	0.4047	hectares

Rounded Measures for Quick Reference

1 oz		= 30 g
4 oz		= 115 g
8 oz		= 225 g
16 oz	= 1 lb	= 450 g
32 oz	= 2 lb	= 900 g
36 oz	= 2¼ lb	= 1000 g (1 kg)
1 c	= 8 oz	= 250 ml
2 c (1 pt)	= 16 oz	= 500 ml
4 c (1 qt)	= 32 oz	= 1 liter
4 qt (1 gal)	= 128 oz	= 3¾ liter
⅜ in.		= 1.0 cm
1 in.		= 2.5 cm
2 in.		= 5.0 cm
2½ in.		= 6.5 cm
12 in. (1 ft)		= 30 cm
1 yd		= 90 cm
100 ft		= 30 m
1 mi		= 1.6 km
32° F		= 0° C
212° F		= 100° C
1 in.^{2}		= 6.5 cm^2
1 ft^2		= 930 cm^2
1 yd^2		= 8360 cm^2
1 a.		= 4050 m^2